All Rights For All

WORKING FOR JUSTICE

Rose O'Keefe

Copyright © 2023 Rose O'Keefe

All rights reserved under International and Pan-American Copyright Conventions. Except for brief quotations in articles and reviews, no part of this book may be reproduced or transmitted in any form without prior written permission from the publisher, R. O'Keefe, 217 Gregory St., Rochester, NY 14620. rokeefehistory.com

ISBN: 978-1-7377803-5-9 (paperback)
ISBN: 978-1-7377803-4-2 (ebook)

This work is dedicated to my brother, David F. O'Keefe, (1942–2023) and my sister, Julie A. O'Keefe (1945–2014).

Acknowledgements

Kindness goes a long way to smooth the path of a project like this. I started researching local history before my first book, *Rochester's South Wedge,* came out in 2005. Professionals, such as the late Karl Kabelac, of the special collection department of the University of Rochester, the late Leah Kemp from the Rochester Museum & Science Center, the late Ann Salter from the Rochester Historical Society, Cynthia Howk from the Landmark Society, Richard Reisem from Friends of Mount Hope Cemetery, and librarians at the Local History & Genealogy Division of the Rochester Public Library, were helpful and kind.

In 2008 I joined two groups that have had an impact on my confidence and career: Toastmasters International and Rochester Area Children's Writers and Illustrators. The members of TM Life Learners Club varied from seasoned speakers to newbies. RACWI members include award winners, seasoned fiction and non-fiction authors and illustrators, and newbies of all ages and genres. Both have been safe places to learn and grow. Special thanks go to TM's D'Lores Simmons, "The Story Teach'a."

More recently, in 2018, kind words from noted scholars Celeste-Marie Bernier, Ka'mal McClarin, Leigh Fought, and David Blight, kept me humming along. Consultant Laura Thorne of Wildebeest Publishing Co. has stayed with me through the learning curve. Women in my writing group, Rosa Dratsch, Joanne Insull, Marile Waterstraat, Paula Weld-Cary, and Valerie McPherson gave me honest feedback. Copyediting from Ronda Roaring at Ronda Roaring Communications was invaluable. An anonymous gentle reader restored my smile many times and Marcella Richer, a history-buff beta reader, gave me excellent suggestions.

Contents

Acknowledgements	v
Chronology	ix
Preface	xvii
Introduction	xix
Chapter 1: Bondage in Maryland	1
Chapter 2: The Baly Family Ancestry	4
Chapter 3: The Lloyd Family	8
Chapter 4: Young Frederick's Father	10
Chapter 5: The Great House	13
Chapter 6: Young Frederick's Mother	15
Chapter 7: Wye Plantation	17
Chapter 8: Baltimore	19
Chapter 9: The Auld Family	22
Chapter 10: Cast His Cares	25
Chapter 11: Economic Slump	27
Chapter 12: Farm Work	30
Chapter 13: Apprenticeship	34
Chapter 14: Betterment	36
Chapter 15: The Murray Family	38
Chapter 16: Plans for Escape	42
Chapter 17: An Abolitionist's Life	44
Chapter 18: New Bedford, Massachusetts	46
Chapter 19: A New Community	49
Chapter 20: Not an Exhibit	56
Chapter 21: Attacks against Hypocrisy	62
Chapter 22: Personal vs. Public Life	64
Chapter 23: The Abolitionists's Circle	67

Chapter 24: An Ambitious Undertaking	72
Chapter 25: Happiness of Home	80
Chapter 26: Travel Abroad	83
Afterword	85
About the Author	87
Index	89

Chronology

In addition to sources cited in the *All Rights for All* manuscript, general information in this timeline is compiled from the chronology in Dickson J. Preston's *Young Frederick Douglass*, the National Park Service website and the Internet.

The harsh legacy of slavery is passed down for centuries by different cultures.

1649: Edward Lloyd II's father, a white planter, merchant, and politician born in Virginia, moves to Maryland.

1671: Edward Lloyd II born at Wye House, Talbot County, Maryland. He later inherits his father's house and land.

1690: By this year, the island colony of Barbados, population 60,000 Black slaves and 20,000 whites, supplies the mainland with Black workers trained under harsh codes.

1696: Edward Lloyd II inherits his grandfather's Wye River residence and lands. A year later he receives 250 acres from his mother's estate.

1701: First generation Baly, paternal ancestor of Frederick Bailey (Douglass), born, Talbot County, Maryland.

1719: Edward Lloyd dies, leaves his Talbot County estate of about 7,000 acres, cash, 108,283 pounds of tobacco; 17 indentured servants, 30 slaves, two vessels, and more.

1720 (c.): Sue and Selah Baly, first generation maternal ancestors of F. Bailey, born, Skinner Plantation, Talbot County, which is worked by white indentured servants. No record shows when the Skinners became slave owners or when Baly family members were willed to descendants of the Skinner family.

1742: Slave ship brings first slaves from Africa to Talbot County. Before then small lots, usually from Barbados, arrive as trade for Eastern Shore tobacco, timber and fur.

1745: Jenny, Baly second generation, great-grandmother of F. Bailey, born, Skinner Plantation, Talbot County.

1767: Aaron Anthony, seventh of poor white farmers, born, Talbot County.

1774: Betsey, Baly third generation, grandmother of F. Bailey, born, Skinner Plantation, Talbot County.

1776: Quakers in Talbot County forbid slave ownership after 1776.

1779: Edward Lloyd V, born, Wye House, Talbot County, into wealthy Eastern Shore family. He serves as Governor from 1809 to 1811 and U. S. Senator from 1819 to 1826.

1792: Harriet, Baly fourth generation, mother of F. Bailey, born, Skinner Plantation.

1793: Lucretia Coffin, second child born to Quakers in Nantucket, Massachusetts. Her father, is a whale-fisherman and her mother runs the family mercantile business.

1797: Aaron Anthony marries into the Skinner family and moves slaves, including Betsey and Harriet, to Holme Hill Farm on Tuckahoe Creek, Talbot County. A few years later, he makes a list of the names, ages and mothers of his slaves.

1800: John Brown, the fourth of eight children, born in Torrington, Connecticut. He is a fervent white Christian who feels guided to end American slavery as a sacred duty.

1804: Thomas James, born into slavery in Canajoharie, New York. He renames himself after taking his liberty and becomes an African Methodist Episcopal Zion minister, abolitionist, administrator and author.

1805: William Lloyd Garrison born, Newburyport, Massachusetts into a struggling white family. After working as an apprentice at a local paper and writing anonymous articles, he becomes involved in the anti-slavery movement in the 1820s.

1806: Maria Weston born, Weymouth, Massachusetts, oldest of eight in a middle-class white family. As a girl, she receives a strong education while living in England.

1810: David Ruggles, first of eight children, born Norwich, Connecticut, to free Black parents. He attends religious charity schools in Norwich.

1811: Wendell Phillips, born to a wealthy white family in Boston. He becomes a member of Boston reformers' inner circle, an ardent abolitionist and Susan B. Anthony's mentor.

1811: Abby Kelley, born a white Quaker, Pelham, Massachusetts and grows up in Worcester, Massachusetts, at a time when women are to be silent and obedient.

1812: James McCune Smith, born into slavery in Manhattan, son of a Black woman born into slavery in South Carolina, and a white merchant who was her mother's owner. He is set free by the Emancipation Act of New York in 1827.

1813 (c.): Anna Murray, one of 13 Black children, the first one born free in Denton, Maryland. Later marries Frederick Bailey and is the mother of their five children.

1818: Aaron Anthony's records show Frederick Augustus Washington Bailey born, Holme Hill Farm, Talbot County, Maryland, in February.

1820: U.S. Congress outlaws the slave trade as piracy, but the profits are so great that this law is ignored in some states.

1821: Lucretia C. Mott becomes a Quaker minister, one of a rare group of women who travel as part of their outreach.

1822(c.,): Harriet Tubman, birth name Araminta Ross, born to slave parents on a large plantation in Dorchester County, Maryland. At age 5 or 6, she works doing childcare and is regularly whipped.

1824: Frederick B. is sent to the home of his master, A. Anthony, with Anthony's daughter and son-in-law, Lucretia and Thomas Auld and meets siblings and cousins.

1825: Frederick B.'s mother, Harriet, visits him for the last time. After his aunt and uncle flee that summer, Frederick hears about escape to free states for the first time.

1826: Frederick B. is sent to care for Hugh and Sophia Auld's son, in Fells Point in Baltimore, in March. His master, A. Anthony dies in November.

1827: When A. Anthony's slaves are divided among his heirs, Frederick B. is awarded to Thomas Auld and returns to Baltimore where Sophia Auld teaches him to spell.

1828: Wm. L. Garrison's skills as a newspaper writer, lead to his appointment as editor of the first American journal to promote legally-mandated temperance.

1828: Maria Weston returns to Boston to serve as principal of a new, progressive girls' high school. She leaves teaching two years later to marry Henry Chapman.

1830: Wm. L. Garrison's demand for immediate emancipation gets him labeled as an extremist. Also, Lucretia Mott is supported by her husband not to buy products made by slave labor. He is a merchant who stops his trade in cotton around 1830.

1831: Wm. L. Garrison publishes the first issue of *The Liberator* on January 1. He forms the New England Anti-Slavery Society. Georgia offers a reward for his kidnapping.

1830-31: Anna Murray, her sisters, Elizabeth and Charlotte, and her brother, Philip, move to Baltimore.

1832: After a religious awakening, Frederick Bailey joins an A.M.E. church. He secretly buys a copy of *The Columbian Orator*, and studies its inspirational speeches diligently.

1833: Frederick is sent St. Michaels, Talbot County, to work for Thomas Auld. He lives with his cousin, aunt, and sister, and often goes hungry. He organizes a Sunday school for young Black men that white men break up. Auld decides to rent him out.

1833: Wm. L. Garrison founds the American Anti-Slavery Society to which L. Mott attends as a guest. Maria W. Chapman, with sisters Caroline, Deborah and Anne Weston and others, found the Boston Female Anti-Slavery Society.

1834: Frederick B. begins the year as field hand under Edward Covey, a cruel slave breaker. In August he fights with Covey and is no longer whipped.

1834: Edward Lloyd V dies in June and is buried in the family grounds at Wye House.

1835: Frederick B. starts the year working as field hand for William Freeland and teaches reading at a Sunday school for 20 to 40 other slaves. Anna Murray starts working for Francis and Elizabeth Montell, in Fells Point, Baltimore.

1836: Frederick B. and others try to escape, fail and are jailed in Easton, Talbot County. He is sent back to Baltimore to Hugh and Sophia Auld, trains as a caulker and is badly beaten by white apprentices. He no longer accepts the attitude of some Black church leaders against abolitionist like Wm. L. Garrison and the American Anti-Slavery Society.

1837: Frederick B. joins a debating club of young, free Black men in Baltimore, and he meets Anna Murray, a housekeeper, and the free Black daughter of a former slave.

1837: Wendell Phillips devotes himself fulltime to the anti-slavery cause after the murder of abolitionist editor Elijah Lovejoy.

1838: Frederick B. flees on Sept. 3, and travels by train, ferry and steamboat to Philadelphia, then a train and ferry to New York City, where he calls himself Frederick Johnson. He reaches David Ruggles who edits the *Mirror of Liberty*, the first Black-owned and Black-run magazine in the nation.

1838: Frederick Bailey and Anna Murray are married Sept. 15. They take Johnson as their last name and travel to New Bedford, Massachusetts, where he plans to work as a caulker. They room with a Black couple, Mary and Nathan Johnson, and at N. Johnson's suggestion, Frederick changes his last name to Douglass. He begins a subscription to *The Liberator* and joins Zion chapel, an African Methodist Episcopal Zion.

1839: F. Douglass first hears Wm. L. Garrison, Wendell Phillips, and other abolitionist leaders; is inspired by abolitionism, and is a regular speaker at A.M.E. Zion Church. In March, he gives his first publicly recorded speech as one of ten Blacks who speak out against colonization, and he praises Wm. L. Garrison and *The Liberator*. Frederick and Anna welcome their first child, Rosetta, in June.

1840: Frederick and Anna welcome their first son, Lewis Henry, in July.

1840: L. Mott is one of six women delegates at the World's Anti-Slavery Convention, in London, where, beforehand, the men vote to limit the American women's participation, and for female delegates to sit separately. Mott meets Elizabeth Cady Stanton there.

1840-43. F. Douglass travels across New England for the Rhode Island and Massachusetts anti-slavery societies, for four years.

1841: After F. Douglass gives a vivid account of his life to about a thousand abolitionists at the annual meeting of the Massachusetts Anti-Slavery Society in Nantucket, in August, Society agent John A. Collins, urges Douglass to become one of his assistants. Douglass shares the facts about his life with Wm. L. Garrison and Wendell Philips.

1841: Quaker abolitionist Abby Kelley's election to the board of A.A.S.S. causes a disruption. Stephen S. Foster, Parker Pillsbury, Abby Kelley, James Monroe, and Frederick Douglass lead the Rhode Island campaign against slavery. Douglass may have met activist Elizabeth Cady Stanton at a meeting of the Boston Female Anti-Slavery Society; he goes on crusade through New York State with others, including Kelley, one of a few women lecturers.

1841: In September, F. Douglass and J. Collins are evicted from local trains. That fall the Douglass family moves from New Bedford to Lynn, Massachusetts. His first speech, in Lynn, reports in detail his attacks against Southern slavery and Northern Racism.

1842: F. Douglass is hired in January as an anti-slavery lecturer after a successful tour. Anna gives birth to Fred Jr. in March. From late March to early May, F. D. speaks in 40 eastern and central Massachusetts towns.

1842: Lucretia Mott attends Anti-Sabbath Convention in Boston organized by Wm. L. Garrison, and then the A.A.S.S.'s annual meeting in NYC and gives a controversial speech. At the convention, F. Douglass, W. Phillips, and A. Kelley introduce a resolution to dissolve the American Union.

1842: A. Kelley, in high demand as a speaker, and F. Douglass address meetings in 19 towns across New York; they meet radical Quakers Isaac and Amy Post in Rochester.

1842: Douglass addresses meetings supporting fugitive George Latimer. Wm. L. Garrison, W. Phillips, F. Douglass, and Charles Remond speak at rallies across New England. Douglass writes his first public letter, supporting George Latimer.

1842-1843: F. Douglass travels across New England and New York State, and often experiences Northern racism.

1843: After the American Anti-Slavery Society sets goal of holding 100 anti-slavery meetings, Douglass volunteers and travels in New England, upstate New York, Ohio, Indiana, and Pennsylvania, with George Bradburn, John Collins, James Monroe, Sidney Howard Gay, and Charles Remond.

1844: F. Douglass and Wm. L. Garrison continue to collaborate. Douglass meets Ruth Cox on tour, claims her as his sister and brings her home to New Bedford in the fall.

1844: Frederick and Anna welcome the birth of their son, Charles, in October. Douglass starts his first autobiography at home.

1845: *Narrative of a Slave* publicized at Anti-Slavery Convention in New York City in May; is published in Boston in June. F. Douglass, J. Buffam and Hutchinson Singers sail to Liverpool in August. Douglass writes of arriving on "visit to the home of my paternal ancestors."

Preface

The harsh legacy of slavery was passed down for centuries by different cultures. This study shares the contribution of famous and lesser known women and men whose good deeds added to the drive to end this horrid practice.

"All Rights for All" was the motto of *Frederick Douglass' Paper*, the new abolitionist paper Douglass created by merger with Gerrit Smith's Liberty Party paper in June 1851.

While Douglass's life story and works have been shared many times, the efforts of other activists and agitators have not been shared as widely. These activists sought the fresh air of freedom, the sunshine of personal happiness and the friendship of allies to counter the stench of slavery, the darkness of hatred and the animosity of enemies.

Introduction

Slavery existed in North America for centuries. So, why did I learn so little about it in school? Voracious reading as a child never taught me how widespread slavery was around the world or in the Americas. One time, as I glanced through the shelves of a local library, I came upon a surprising new book, *The Other Slavery: The Uncovered Story of Indian Enslavement in America*. The author, Andrés Reséndez, explained that, when early European explorers arrived, they saw native tribes giving prisoners of war to Europeans as guides, guards, and interpreters, in exchange for weapons and horses.

Between 1670 and 1720, Reséndez wrote, European colonizers in the Carolinas exported more native peoples to the Caribbean than they imported Africans. When French explorers arrived in what is now eastern Canada, they traded thousands of native slaves around what is now Quebec City and Montreal. As French explorers moved further inland, they came across such a vast network of natives selling others for guns and ammunition all across North America that it astounded them. "Colonial Americans in places such as New England, Virginia, and the Carolinas had Indian slaves in the seventeenth and eighteenth centuries. But the institution was subsequently eclipsed by African slavery. By the middle of the nineteenth century, the memory of these earlier Indian slaves had been . . . erased."[1]

Why do those past injustices matter today?

Dr. Joy DeGruy argued in her book, *Post Traumatic Slave Syndrome: America's Legacy of Enduring Injury and Healing*, that they matter very much: While humans have enslaved others for centuries all around the globe, slavery as practiced in the colonies and the United States was a harsher form than others. So, let's go

---

[1] Andrés Reséndez, *The Other Slavery: The Uncovered Story of Indian Enslavement in America* (Boston: Houghton, Mifflin, Harcourt, 2016), 172–173, and 331 (note 2).

back to the first captive Africans, who were shipped to Portugal in the 1400s, and their descendants, who were brought to South Carolina in the 1500s.

It's estimated that the number of Africans who died in transit to the West Indies, Brazil, Europe, and the New World is greater than the number of Jews who died during the Holocaust years. In 2016, the United Nations recommended the United States admit that the transatlantic slave trade was a crime against humanity.[2]

According to Yuval Noah Harari, in his book, *Sapiens: A Brief History of Humankind*, the circular thinking that fostered beliefs about one caste or culture being less pure than others set up a devasting racial hierarchy in the sixteenth to eighteenth centuries in the Americas. European traders imported slaves from Africa because it was cheaper than importing them from Asia.

Africa already had networks that sold slaves, mostly to the Middle East, so traders had no need to start one from the ground up. Plantations in places like Virginia, the Caribbean, and Brazil had malaria and yellow fever, which existed in Africa and from which Africans had some immunity.[3]

In the Tidewater region, the areas of southeast Virginia, northeastern North Carolina, parts of Maryland facing the Chesapeake, and the Deep South, slavery anchored the economy and culture, according to Colin Woodard, in his book *American Nations: A History of the Eleven Rival Regional Cultures of North America*. At first, colonial slave owners, who favored the English monarchy, imported poor black and white men and women as indentured servants, who could earn their freedom, if they survived the term of servitude. Some early black servants then lived freely, owned land, hired servants, held public office, and married. These freedoms faded after 1660 as owners followed the practices of the West Indies and Deep South, and legalized horrific slave codes imported from the British colony of Barbados in 1698. From this time, owners

---

[2] Dr. Joy DeGruy, *Post Traumatic Slave Syndrome: America's Legacy of Enduring Injury and Healing* (Portland, Oregon: Joy DeGruy Publications, 2005), 57.

[3] Yuval Noah Harari, *Sapiens: A Brief History of Humankind*. (New York: Harper, 2015), 140.

considered African adults and children brought to Virginia and Maryland as permanent slaves.[4]

The Virginia Slave Code of 1705 absolved slave owners of the legal consequences for killing a slave who resisted the "master, owner or other person, by his or her order . . . but the master, owner and every such other person so giving correction, shall be free and acquit of all punishment and accusation for the same, as if such accident had never happened." It was legal to kill a slave who raised "a hand against any Christian," wrote DeGruy.[5]

Those injustices matter today because the dark deeds of the past still cast shadows. No matter the era, some people have always treated others with dignity and respect. Eventually, this behavior grew into the great drive in the nineteenth century for All Rights for All.

---

[4] Colin Woodard, *American Nations: A History of the Eleven Rival Regional Cultures of North America*. (New York: Penguin Group, 2011) 86-87.

[5] DeGruy, *Post Traumatic Slave Syndrome*, 47, and 59.

CHAPTER 1

Bondage in Maryland

The English adventurers who settled in Talbot County, Maryland, made their county seat a hub of social and business activities, according to Dickson J. Preston in his book, *Young Frederick Douglass, The Maryland Years*. Within a few decades after receiving large land grants, these founders formed a close-knit aristocracy described as "the purest ever existing in America." Their wealth came from land ownership and from tobacco farmed with cheap forced labor.

At first these workers were immigrants from London's slums, convicts from British prisons, and Irish and Scottish rebels, who the owners believed were superior workers. But gradually, black slaves from Barbados replaced European workers.

The children of slaves, who had come to Talbot County before 1750, had grown up in the West Indies since the early 1600s, according to Preston. These West Indians, mostly from Barbados, traveled by ship on deck along with rum, sugar, molasses, and salt. They formed their own creole culture that changed them into Americanized Africans, different from native Africans. Their maternal traditions and values didn't match those of later slaves in the Deep South with whom they had little other than skin color in common.[1]

Large plantations didn't exist in the early 1700s, and most slave families in Talbot County lived near their owners. Slave women worked as cooks, house servants, nurses, and, at times, field hands. The owning family was usually a

---

[1] Dickson J. Preston, *Young Frederick Douglass: The Maryland Years* (Baltimore: Johns Hopkins University Press, 1980), 10–11.

couple with their children, a few elderly relatives, and fewer than five slaves, Preston wrote. The English slave laws used by colonial owners were harsher than the laws for whites and demanded death by hanging for stealing a loaf of bread. Frederick Douglass's Baly ancestors saw unspeakable cruelties, including a brutal punishment in 1745, the year his great-grandmother, Jenny Baly, was born, Preston wrote.[2]

It was common, particularly around Chesapeake Bay, for healthy slave women to bear children for the owner's inventory. These women's lives were like those of others on the plantation, but they had the added duty of bearing a child every two years, with no control over who fathered them, wrote Lydia Bjornlund in *Women of Colonial America*. Because children had no value on the slave market until they were able to work to pay for their keep, they often stayed with their mothers until they were ten. Nursing mothers took their babies into the fields for up to three years. These women didn't receive the harsh punishments of other adult slaves and were less likely than men to be sold.

Despite forced pregnancies, these hard-working women were heads of their own households and often models of stability and self-reliance. They sold poultry, eggs, pies, cakes, produce, and handcrafted items, including baskets. They hunted, trapped, or pilfered meat, and sold their goods around their own plantation and to other plantations, in an active slave economy.[3]

Manumission, the release from slavery, was popular after the American Revolution, particularly in Talbot County, where Quaker rules forbade slave ownership after 1776, Preston wrote. There were more free blacks in Talbot County than any other county in Maryland, according to Kate Clifford Larson in *Bound for the Promised Land: Harriet Tubman*, and by 1790, Quaker meetings on the Eastern Shore had no slave owners in attendance.[4]

---

[2] Preston, *Young F. D.*, 13, 14.

[3] Lydia Bjornlund, *Women in History: Women of Colonial America* (Farmington Hills, Michigan: Lucent Books, 2004), 47–49.

[4] Preston, *Young F. D.*, 17–19; and Kate Clifford Larson, *Bound for the Promised Land: Harriet Tubman* (New York: One World Ballantine, 2004), 81.

Under Maryland law, the bi-racial children of one black and one known white parent had special status, that other blacks didn't have as white fathers could acknowledge in their wills their bi-racial children, according to Preston. Children born of white women served for seven years; those of black women were enslaved for life, but if those children were freed, they could testify in court.[5] Those practices may seem like legal technicalities, but they applied directly to people, such as young Frederick's mother, Harriet Bailey, and his grandmother, Betsey Bailey.

---

[5] Preston, *Young F. D.*, 13 (note 38).

CHAPTER 2

The Baly Family Ancestry

Preston included a list in the chronology of Baly ancestors including Jenny Baly (b.1745), Jenny's daughter Betsey (b.1774), Jenny's granddaughter, Harriet Bailey (b. 1792), and Harriet's children—Perry, Sarah, Eliza, Frederick, Kitty, Ariana, and Harriet. Preston found papers documenting six generations of young Frederick's family tree dating back to the early 1700s when a man named Baly arrived in Talbot County. Owners counted their slave workers the same way they kept records of farm animals and household goods. Over the years, whether the owner of the plantation on which Frederick Douglass was born had been the Anthony, the Skinner, or the Rice family, there had been a person named Baly, Bealy, Bail, Baley, or Baily for five generations, when the spelling *Bailey* showed up in the records during the Lloyd family's ownership of the plantation.

The Baileys raised their children in a family circle that valued self-reliance, independence, strength of character, and respect for maternal ancestors. The Bailey family lived in "peaceful poverty and ignorance" on the land of one of the wealthiest slave-owning plantations in the colonies, Preston wrote. The owners claimed they never harmed their slave workers. They could justify this claim because, while they partied in the state capital at Annapolis, called the "giddiest capital" in the colonies, it was the overseers, and not the owners, who did the harsh work of controlling slaves.[6]

Although Frederick Douglass never knew his own birth date, records found by Preston showed young Frederick's family line going back to 1701, the birth

---

[6] Preston, *Young F. D.*, 13, 16–17, and 205.

year of his grandmother's grandfather. In the 1700s, the family lived in the most prosperous and populated area of the colony of Maryland's Eastern Shore. By the time of Frederick's birth in 1818, the Baileys were a settled black subculture of former West Indians, unlike new captives arriving from Africa. Young Frederick's master, Aaron Anthony, used to call him his "little Indian boy". Years later, Frederick's son, Lewis, wrote to his father, after having visited relatives on the Eastern Shore. These relatives told Lewis that his father's grandmother, Betsey Bailey, was of Indian descent.[7]

It was common in Maryland to keep black slave families together as wealthy owners bred them like prized livestock. Early owners kept lists of their slaves' names along with the names of their horses. The Bailey family's strength as a clan had deep roots in traditional life in Africa. Even though they were forced to be loyal to their master, they honored their families by passing on certain names to their children such as variations of Betty and Harry and passed them "from generation to generation like family heirlooms."[8]

In 1797, according to Preston, young Frederick's grandparents, Isaac Bailey, who was free, and Betsey, who was a slave belonging to the Lloyds, set up house on the Lloyd estate near Tuckahoe Creek, away from the slave quarters, in a clearing in the woods. Their windowless one-room cabin had a packed clay floor, a mud and straw chimney, and a ladder to an attic. The site had a shallow well and was close to a spring that went through a ravine toward a spot called "muddy shore" where they trapped shad and herring in nets during the spring runs.

The trees along Tuckahoe Creek included oaks, maples, sweet gums, walnuts, and loblolly or southern yellow pines. Isaac Bailey was a woodcutter, who earned his income selling trimmed hardwood and pine to carpenters and cabinetmakers.[9] During the thirty years Isaac Bailey worked as a woodcutter, his

---

[7] Preston, *Young F. D.*, 6–9, and 214 (note 22).
[8] Preston, *Young F. D.*, 5, 6.
[9] Burchard, *Frederick Douglass: For the Great Family of Man* (New York: Atheneum, 2003), 8, and Preston, *Young F. D.*, 17.

business did so well that he was able to hire a slave by the year at least twice. The 1820 United States census listed Isaac Bailey as a free, colored male aged forty-five, head of household living with nine children (three boys and six girls, all under the age of fourteen), and three women, including Betsey, who was forty-six and nine months pregnant with her last child.[10]

Betsey continued to live in the cabin after Isaac's death and the removal of her children and grandchildren, until she became weak and blind. Some whites and blacks called her cabin "Aunt Bettie's Lot" for years.[11] "Aunt Betsey's modest cabin near the Tuckahoe was a sort of nursery where slave children lived in blissful ignorance of what lay in store for them," Burchard wrote. It was home to many children, mostly belonging to Betsey's daughters—Jenny, Esther, Milly, Priscilla, and Harriet—all of whom worked far enough away to keep them from visiting often. This small cabin was a haven for many children, including young Frederick, who dearly loved both of his grandparents. As was normal for young slave children, he had a long shirt to wear and, if he avoided the tougher, older slave boys, he was happy.[12]

In his autobiographies, Douglass wrote about how he fished in the creek with a bent pin or linger near a nearby water mill, watching the heavy wheel turn to grind corn into meal for a constant stream of customers. Even though the children lived on cornmeal, with a piece of sweet potato or crabmeat now and then, none of the children under Betsey's care ever starved. It was the only home young Frederick ever had, and he loved it. Locals respected Betsey as a nurse, as a skilled farmer because of her success with sweet potatoes, and as a craftswoman for the fishnets she wove that were in great demand.[13] Douglass wrote in his second autobiography, *My Bondage and My Freedom*, that the first

---

[10] Preston, *Young F. D.*, 18 and 216 (note 53).

[11] Preston, *Young F. D.*, 17–18.

[12] Burchard, *F. Douglass*, 10; and Frederick Douglass, *The Frederick Douglass Papers*. Series two, Autobiographical Writings, vol. 2 (New Haven: Yale University Press, 2003), 24–25.

[13] Burchard, *F. Douglass*, 10–11; and Douglass, *F. D. Papers*. Series two, Autobiographical Writings, vol. 2, 22–24.

eight years of his life were carefree. He described his birthplace as surrounded by a shabby white neighborhood.[14]

Betsey Bailey was a "tall, straight-backed and strong, more brown than black" woman who had "remarkable self-reliance and independence of mind," Preston wrote in *Young Frederick Douglass*. She passed these characteristics on to her children. Her owner/master, Aaron Anthony, paid her $2.40 ($59 in 2022) per birth for her services as a midwife and didn't hire her out as a field hand as he did her daughters. In 1809, he paid her $26.50 ($638 in 2022) for eleven births.[15]

The trade-off Betsey made for living with a free black man in a remote area was taking care of all the infants in the Bailey family, in addition to her own children. Frederick grew up with his grandmother's youngest children and several cousins, whose mothers worked in Aaron Anthony's fields or were hired out to others. The Lloyds didn't provide Betsey with extra rations of corn for the care of the children, so she supported them before they were old enough to use a hoe or work fishnets with her. Despite the hardships, Douglass later described her home as "spirited, joyous, uproarious, and happy."[16]

---

[14] Douglass, *F. D. Papers*. Series two, Autobiographical Writings, vol. 2, 21.

[15] Preston, *Young F. D.*, 17, 19–20; Frederick Douglass, The Frederick Douglass Papers. Series three, Correspondence, vol. 1, 1842–1852 (New Haven: Yale University Press, 2009), 317 (note 13); and U.S. Inflation Calculator 1635–2022: https://www.in2013dollars.com; for 1809.

[16] William McFeely, *Frederick Douglass* (New York: Norton, 1991), 8–9.

CHAPTER 3

The Lloyd Family

In the years since the Edward Lloyd family arrived from Wales to Maryland's Eastern Shore in the 1660s, the family owned its own mansion, outbuildings, highly prized thoroughbreds, and about seven hundred sheep. By the early 1800s, Colonel Edward Lloyd V was one of the most successful farmers in Maryland. Locals considered him "a demi-god to the slaves."[17] Preston wrote that, since the Lloyd family's arrival, its wealth came from the slave labor that produced tobacco, wheat, corn, rye, and from political ties. The Lloyds never sold slaves; never gave them their freedom; gave them the least amount of food, clothing, and shelter; and worked them under harsh overseers.[18]

Colonel Lloyd's political career came second to managing an estate of almost ten thousand acres on thirteen farms. Although he had been Maryland governor three times and state senator twice, he loved horses more than people. His nickname was "Lord Cock-de-doodle-do" for his passion for cockfighting. When tobacco crops failed in 1825, Lloyd planted wheat. He became the biggest wheat farmer in Maryland, and one of the biggest in the country. Among his possessions was a collection of silver so large that, even after it was looted during the American Revolution, it was still vast.[19]

During the years when young Frederick lived in the backwoods, Colonel Lloyd's plantation was a city unto itself. Lloyd ran his many farms with a strict order that had been developed over a hundred years. The main farm and mansion

---

[17] Burchard, *F. Douglass*, 13–14.
[18] Preston, *Young F. D.*, 42–43; and Burchard, *F. Douglass*, 13–14, 21.
[19] Preston, *Young F. D.*, 42–43, and 45–47.

were at the center of smoke-, milk-, and icehouses; outbuildings for a blacksmith, carpenter, shoemaker, and wheelwright; a private dock; and a windmill. Lloyd owned a dozen other farms and kept buying more. In the 1820s, he owned 170 slaves and delegated an overseer rated for his efficiency, for each farm. Lloyd and his well-to-do guests never socialized with Anthony, who never mingled with other overseers, who in turn, scorned the slaves.[20]

---

[20] Preston, *Young F. D.*, 48, 60.

CHAPTER 4

Young Frederick's Father

Aaron Anthony, according to Preston, was the dirt-poor son of a lowly tenant farmer and learned his letters and numbers while working on boats that hauled cargo to the Chesapeake Bay. He did so well at hauling cargo that he became captain of the *Elizabeth Ann*, owned by Lloyd. For three years, Anthony transported the Lloyd family from their mansion to their Annapolis townhouse.

Anthony worked hard and, in early 1797, moved up by marrying Ann Skinner, who was from a prominent Talbot County family and the descendent of a Mayflower family. Lloyd set them up in a rent-free house on his property and gave Anthony a raise. Aaron Anthony invested his money and bought Holme Hill Farm from Lloyd in 1802. In 1805, Anthony bought 150 neighboring acres that became Red House Farm. In 1806, he bought forty-one acres of swamp land where the Bailey's cabin stood. He never bought slaves but owned thirty at the time of his death.[21]

Sometime after his marriage to Ann Skinner in 1798, according to Preston, Aaron Anthony wrote, in a private document called "My Black People," a list of the names and ages of the slave workers he came to own through marriage. Anthony's descendants updated the list for several decades, making it an unprecedented record of slaveholdings from colonial days on. That document confirmed Frederick Bailey's birth in February 1818.

In 1826, when Aaron Anthony died, Preston wrote that two Bailey family subgroups emerged, and an updated list pulled together information from

---

[21] Preston, *Young F. D.*, 26–27.

several sources that Frederick Bailey's great-grandmother was the same Jinny, Jenny, and Jeney. It revealed details Douglass never learned in his lifetime. Contrary to his understanding that his grandmother Betsey and grandfather Isaac had five daughters and a son, they actually had nine daughters, three sons, and about twenty-five grandchildren. Anthony's thirty home-bred slaves were valued at $3,065 ($91,737 in 2022). The list, showing Douglass's mother's birthdate in February 1792, also showed five other children Harriet Bailey bore in addition to Frederick.[22]

In his 1845 autobiography, *Narrative of the Life of Frederick Douglass, an American Slave, Written by Himself*, Douglass wrote that his white master/owner "Captain" Anthony, was said to be in fact his father. After 1816, Anthony had stopped hiring Harriet Bailey out to work in the fields. Instead, she lived on Holme Hill and was hired out to its tenant farmer. It was common practice that, before some slave babies reached their first birthday, they were taken from their mothers and given to a woman who had become too old to work in the fields. Since Harriet Bailey already had little contact with her older children, she and Frederick had little time together, and he barely remembered her.[23]

According to Preston, the name Frederick Augustus Washington Bailey came about in part because Augustus had been a son of Betsey's who had died, and Bailey was his mother's family name. His color was lighter than his mother's or grandmother's, of a light tan shade called yellow, and his looks made others beside his owner who saw him, think of an Indian boy. Anthony never admitted to being Frederick's father, and Frederick never got the legal status granted to the child of a white father and black mother.[24]

The term mulatto, comes from the Spanish for young mule, the offspring of a female horse and a jackass. It refers to the children of one black and one known white parent.[25] Frederick Douglass later wrote, ". . . the fact remains, in all

---

[22] Preston, *Young F. D.*, 8 and 27; and U.S. Inflation Calculator for 1826.

[23] Frederick Douglass, *The Frederick Douglass Papers*. Series two, Autobiographical Writings, vol. 1 (New Haven: Yale University Press, 2003), 13.

[24] Preston, *Young F. D.*, 35.

[25] Preston, *Young F. D.*, 13 (note 38).

its glaring odiousness, that slaveholders have ordained, and by law established, that the children of slave women shall in all cases follow the condition of their mothers."[26]

Aaron Anthony measured the food and counted the clothing for the field workers from the central farm. As an adult, Douglass remembered a monthly allotment of eight pounds of pickled pork or fish, a bushel of cornmeal, and a pint of salt. The pork or fish was often spoiled and the cornmeal unfit to eat. He didn't recall, maybe because he didn't know, slaves could raise pigs and chickens, tend garden plots, and were allowed to fish and gather clams, oysters, and crabs.[27]

In his second autobiography, *Life and Times of Frederick Douglass Written by Himself,* Douglass listed food and clothing allowances: two tow-linen shirts and one pair of trousers for summer; one woolen trousers and one woolen jacket for winter; one pair of yarn stockings and one pair of shoes for children over age ten. Children under ten were not allotted shoes, stockings, jackets, or trousers—only two coarse tow-linen shirts a year—and went naked when they wore out.[28]

Preston described how, out of sight of the scruffy children, Colonel Lloyd held spectacular parties all summer long for neighboring planters and his circle of friends from Annapolis. He didn't have direct contact with most slaves except for his grooms and house servants—fifteen favored slaves chosen for being good-looking, smart, loyal, and having perfect manners. Burchard noted that these slave servants were at the top of slave society in their spotless clothes. They enjoyed fresh fruits, vegetables, and meat, and looked down on lowly slaves, such as the field hands, who, while out of sight, ate mostly cornmeal and worked and lived in squalor.[29]

---

[26] Douglass, *F. D. Papers. Narrative*, 14.

[27] Preston, *Young F. D.*, 48.

[28] Frederick Douglass, *Autobiographies, Life and Times of Frederick Douglass Written by Himself* (New York: Library of America, 1994), 503–04.

[29] Burchard, *F. Douglass*, 18–19; and Preston, *Young, F. D.*, 49.

CHAPTER 5

The Great House

The contrast couldn't have been more stark between the luxurious Lloyd plantation and Douglass's memories of his backwoods birthplace. During his childhood, locals called Colonel Lloyd's home Wye House or the Great House. When young Frederick left his Grandma Betsey's cabin on Tuckahoe Creek, his memory was of going to a large wood-framed kitchen of a brick house—Aaron Anthony's home—behind Wye House. At the time, Anthony was a widower who lived on the estate with his daughter, Lucretia, and her husband, Thomas Auld.[30]

For the rest of his life, Douglass remembered a morning in 1824 when peaches and pears were ripe on the trees. His grandmother didn't explain where they were going, and he later recalled that he would have given her trouble if she had. As it was, she carried him a few times along the twelve-mile route to Wye Plantation and the Great House.

Their walk ended, going through a service lane called the Long Green Lane that cut through twenty grassy acres, past the slave quarters, to the wharf at Lloyd's Cove. Young Frederick would have had a peek at Wye House, as they headed to a plain red-brick house where "Old Master" Aaron Anthony lived, with a separate kitchen building for the slaves.

Betsey encouraged her grandson to play outside with his brothers, sisters, and cousins. When he found out she had left while he was out back, he fell to the ground crying that she had left without warning. Heartbroken, he curled up and slept alone in a corner of the kitchen.[31] That day he met his brother, Perry,

---

[30] Burchard, *F. Douglass*, 13–15.
[31] Burchard, *F. Douglass*, 14–16; and Preston, *Young F. D.*, 38–39.

sisters Sarah and Eliza, and half a dozen cousins: Phil, Tom, Steve, Jerry, Nancy, and Betty, of all sizes and colors including black, brown, copper, and nearly white, who surrounded him, laughing, yelling, and teasing him.[32] He never got over the shock of his grandmother leaving him at Anthony's house. That loss pained him so deeply that he never fully trusted anyone again.[33]

He had to get used to speaking in a Guinean dialect that he found hard to understand and was surprised to learn that other blacks hadn't lived in Talbot County for as long as his family had. He found out that his master's name was Anthony, usually called Captain Anthony; his brother Perry's name was Cap'n Ant'ney Pey, his cousin's name was Cap'n Ant'ney Tom, and his was Cap'n Ant'ney Fed. He also found out that slaves got whipped for oversleeping more than any other reason.[34]

At age seven, young Frederick's looks were so remarkable that, out of eighty slave children on Colonel Lloyd's central farm, Frederick was chosen as a playmate for Lloyd's youngest son, Daniel.[35] For a time, young Frederick played in the Great House with the twelve-year-old, who seemed not to notice Frederick's color. They roamed the fields, hunting rabbits and birds, with Frederick fetching the kill. Daniel shared cakes and biscuits. He also spared his younger playmate from being bullied by older boys. Later in life, Douglass wrote that his command of the English language came from playing with Daniel and listening to the descriptions of feasts and well-dressed guests at the Great House.

Since he was too young to work in the fields, Frederick also ran errands for Captain Anthony's daughter, Lucretia Auld, tidied the front yard, and drove up the cows in the evening. Auld tended his wounds when he got into fights and rewarded him with bread and butter for singing outside her window. While, as Daniel's companion, young Frederick was neither a field hand nor a house servant, he was given an inside view of the Lloyd family's lavish lifestyle.[36]

---

[32] Preston, *Young F. D.*, 39, 61; and Douglass, *F. D. Papers*. Series two, Autobiographical Writings, vol. 2, 29.

[33] McFeely, *F. D.*, 10.

[34] Preston, *Young F. D.*, 14, 61; and Douglass, *F. D. Papers*. Series two, Autobiographical Writings, vol. 2, 45, 60.

[35] Preston, *Young F. D.*, 54.

[36] Burchard, *F. Douglass*, 22–23; and Preston, *Young F. D.*, 54–55.

CHAPTER 6

Young Frederick's Mother

In addition to the shock of being separated from his grandmother, young Frederick's daily life got worse by being under the care of Aunt Katy, a hot-tempered cook who took care of slave children in the kitchen building on Aaron Anthony's farm. She set out cooled cornmeal mush in a trough, on the kitchen floor or outside, for all the children to eat from like pigs. She didn't like Frederick, favored her children over others, and gave Frederick's food to her own. He had to learn to elbow his way to the trough, scramble for crumbs shaken from the tablecloths, and forage for clams, oysters, crabs, and fish in the creek. Most of the time, the children got thick slabs of cornbread three times a day. One rare time, his mother brought him a heart-shaped ginger cake and, with him perched on her knee, Harriet Bailey yelled at Aunt Katy, making him feel that at least somebody cared about him. It was the last visit the two of them shared, as she died a short time later.[37]

Although he had few visits from his mother, he wrote about her in *My Bondage and My Freedom*, as being "ineffaceably stamped upon my memory. She was tall, and finely proportioned; of a deep black, glossy complexion; had regular features, and, among the other slaves, was remarkably sedate in her manners." As a grown man, seeing pictures of Egyptian royalty reminded him so much of her, he looked at them as if "looking upon the pictures of dear departed ones."[38]

When Harriet Bailey died in 1825 or early 1826, according to Preston, all

---

[37] Douglass, *F. D. Papers*. Series two, Autobiographical Writings, vol. 2, 32–34; Burchard, *F. Douglass*, 18–21; and Preston, *Young F. D.*, 52–53 and 63.

[38] Douglass, *F. D. Papers*. Series two, Autobiographical Writings, vol. 2, 31; and David W. Blight, *Frederick Douglass: Prophet of Freedom* (New York: Simon and Schuster, 2018), 11.

the boy knew about his mother was "that she had suffered a 'long illness"; that she could read, 'the *only* one of all the slaves and colored people in Tuckahoe who enjoyed that advantage"; and she had died without telling him or presumably anyone else, who his father was." Like all who died on that farm, black and white, she was buried in an unmarked grave.

Another memorable event in young Frederick's life happened a few months after his mother's death, Preston wrote, when Harriet's sister, Aunt Jenny, and her husband, Uncle Noah, fled to freedom in the North. Such escapes were risky in the 1820s before the Underground Railroad was in place. Jenny and Noah were both twenty-six years old and had two small children—a seven-year-old girl and a six-year-old boy, whom they left with Betsey Bailey. Until then, Frederick hadn't known there was such a thing as a state where a slave could become free. Anthony offered a reward for them— $50 ($1,497 in 2022) for Jenny and $100 ($2,993 in 2022) for Noah. They must have believed Anthony was going to sell them and separate them because, when Jenny and Noah left the children behind, Anthony sold them to a trader from Alabama.[39]

---

[39] Preston, *Young F. D.*, 64–65; Burchard, *F. Douglass*, 25; and U.S. Inflation Calculator for 1826.

CHAPTER 7

Wye Plantation

Young Frederick's experience with schooling on the Wye Plantation was dreadful. One of the heads of the Copper clan, the largest family group of Lloyd's captive workers, was a crippled man named Isaac, who, in his younger days, had bred fighting cocks for Colonel Lloyd. Uncle Isaac or Doctor Isaac, as he was called, followed a rigid social order and enforced it with four lengths of hickory switches that he used often. After a few bitter sessions learning the lines of the Lord's Prayer by repetition, Frederick avoided the lessons and whippings. Instead he learned as much as he could from his cousin, Tommy, who worked as a cabin boy on the sloop *Sally Lloyd*, and told him about Baltimore, an amazing city beyond the plantation.[40]

When young Frederick was hungry and sang by Lucretia Auld's window, she rewarded him with bread and butter, but Fought wrote in *Women in the World of Frederick Douglass* that to describe her as the kindly daughter of Frederick's master would be simplistic. Auld doled out the rations that were allotted to Aunt Katy, who gave more to her own children than others. If the children had skimpy clothes or no blankets, it was because Auld never gave any to Aunt Katy, whose harshness had Auld's silent approval. Her kindness to young Frederick may have been for a smaller boy who had been picked on by the bigger boys.

According to Fought, most likely Auld wouldn't have noticed Frederick once he outgrew his childishness. Or, it could have been that, when Colonel Lloyd didn't rehire Aaron Anthony in January 1826 and Thomas and Lucretia Auld moved to Hillsboro to open a store, Lucretia decided to send Frederick

---

[40] Burchard, *F. Douglass*, 21; and Preston, *Young F. D.*, 59–61.

to her brother-in-law in Baltimore. Frederick had reached the age where he should be either working on one of Anthony's farms or, as with his brothers and sisters, on another farm in the county. Around that time, Lucretia's sister-in-law, Sophia Auld, asked for help with the care of her son Tommy, who was two, because she was pregnant and due in November. Sophia would have had to advertise and interview a servant on her own, but her brother-in-law had access to more choices. The skills young Frederick had picked up as Daniel Lloyd's playmate and the way he sang were seen as useful for amusing a small child.[41]

There's no way to know if Lucretia Auld favored her light-skinned half-brother, but one day in March 1826, she told him to scrub himself from head to toe and gave him a good pair of pants and a clean white shirt for a trip he would be making to Baltimore. Frederick stayed in the bow of the schooner, which was carrying a large flock of sheep to a slaughterhouse in the city. After docking in Annapolis on the first day, the schooner sailed on to Baltimore. After seeing the city for the first time, Frederick had the excitement of unloading six hundred sheep at Smith's Wharf where he helped drive them to market. Then he walked down lanes and cobbled streets to his new home in Happy Alley, in the shipping neighborhood of Fell's Point.[42]

---

[41] Leigh Fought, *Women in the World of Frederick Douglass* (New York: Oxford University Press, 2017), 30–31.

[42] Burchard, *F. Douglass*, 27–28.

CHAPTER 8

Baltimore

Douglass's main recollection of going to Baltimore was of where he went to live at the bottom of Aliceanna Street, in his new home with the Aulds. There was a large frigate being built close by. At that time, Baltimore, with a total population of about 70,000, had a free black community of about 30,000, many of whom worked on the docks, and the sight of so many blacks must have surprised young Frederick.[43]

Most slaves almost never ate or slept with the people they served. Yet, on his first night in Baltimore, young Frederick ate "a proper supper of meat, cornbread, and milk" with Hugh, Sophia, and Tommy Auld, then climbed to a loft where there was a mattress stuffed with straw, covered with clean sheets and a woolen blanket. Having been taught by her working-class parents that slavery was a crime, Sophia treated Frederick kindly, as if he were her own son. Burchard wrote that, later in life, Douglass was unclear about the year he went to Baltimore but recalled the launching of an eighteen-ton warship in a shipyard where Hugh Auld worked as a ship carpenter. Young Frederick attended the event, which was written up in a May 1826 newspaper.[44]

Frederick's pleasant time with the Aulds lasted until November 1826 when Lucretia Auld's father, Aaron Anthony, died without leaving a will. No one could say whether he would have let Frederick stay in Baltimore,

---

[43] Frederick Douglass, *Narrative of the Life of Frederick Douglass*, introduction and notes by Robert O'Meally (New York: Barnes & Noble Classics, 2003), 109 (note 23); and Preston, *Young F. D.*, 33.

[44] Burchard, *F. Douglass*, 29, and Preston, *Young F. D.*, 84.

so he was sent back to the Lloyd plantation. Anthony's three children—Andrew, Richard, and Lucretia—were to receive a portion of their father's estate.[45]

From his short time around this master, Frederick Bailey described Aaron Anthony as a miserable, anxious man. Anthony's wife had become sickly and died years earlier; their sons didn't do well in life, and there was gossip about Anthony's fondness for Betsey Bailey's attractive daughters. After thirty years of service to Lloyd, Anthony had become violent and inconsistent and wasn't rehired. Lucretia and her husband Thomas Auld had moved to the village of Hillsboro where Thomas ran a store, leaving Anthony alone in his house on the estate.[46]

Anthony died at the age of fifty-nine in Hillsboro while visiting Lucretia, Thomas, and a new granddaughter. The family buried his body in an unmarked grave on Holme Hill Farm not far from that of Harriet Bailey. Without a will, his property would have gone to his daughter and sons, but before the settlement, Lucretia died in July 1827, shortly after giving birth, making her husband heir to her portion.

In October 1827 when young Frederick left Baltimore for the estate settlement, he, Sophia, and Tommy wept bitterly at Fredericks' leaving. After living in the city for over a year, he was out of step with his family in the country. During the dreadful settlement, Frederick watched as Anthony's abusive son, Andrew, kicked Frederick's brother in the head as a threat to all. Lawyers completed the sorting of the slaves for the estate settlement by mid-October 1827 and divided them among the three heirs. They maintained family groups so that Aunt Betsey and four of Harriet Bailey's children stayed in Tuckahoe as property of Andrew; Aunt Katy and her family went to Richard; Thomas Auld received Fredericks's Aunt Milly and her four children, as well as Frederick and his sister, Eliza. To Frederick's relief, Thomas sent him back to Baltimore to live with Hugh and Sophia Auld. The twenty-nine chattel slaves, including babies, were worth $2,800

---

[45] Burchard, *F. Douglass*, 30–31.
[46] Preston, *Young F. D.*, 29–30.

($82,967 in 2022) with each group being worth about $935 ($27,705 in 2022).⁴⁷

Out of Anthony's slaves, Betsey Bailey had borne ten children between 1799 and 1826; her daughter, Milly, had borne seven. Since the exact number of live births and infant deaths was unclear, Betsey's daughter, Harriet, is thought to have borne six children; Jenny, three; young Betty, three; and Hester, one. Another granddaughter also bore seven children during those years, giving Aaron Anthony thirty slaves. In an inventory filed in January 1827 at the Talbot County Courthouse in Easton, these thirty individuals were valued at $3,065 ($90,819 in 2022).⁴⁸ Of Aaron Anthony's slaves, young Frederick's brothers and sisters were in the fifth generation of his Bailey lineage: Perry (b. 1813), Sarah (b. 1814), Eliza (b. 1816), himself (b. 1818), Kitty (b. 1820), Arianna (b. 1822), and Harriet (b. c. 1825).⁴⁹

---

⁴⁷ Burchard, *F. Douglass*, 31–33; McFeely, *F. D.*, 27–29; Fought, *Women*, 31; Preston, *Young F. D.*, 30 and 90–91; and U.S. Inflation Calculator for 1827.

⁴⁸ Preston, *Young F. D.*, 27 and 218 (note 13); and Douglass, *Autobiographies*, 1050.

⁴⁹ Preston, *Young F. D.*, 206.

CHAPTER 9

The Auld Family

As a grown man, Douglass wrote that when he first went to live with the Aulds, Sophia Auld "was a model of affection and tenderness" because she didn't see him as property.[50] Unlike Lucretia Auld, who oversaw slaves, Sophia Auld's family, who were weavers, worked with apprentices who, as bound workers, technically weren't free but weren't property either. Sophia Auld's family hadn't owned slaves, and she hadn't learned how slave-owning families handled slave children. She treated Frederick like a son and saw his desire to read the Bible as a call for salvation. As she tutored him that first year, she gave him self- respect and a love of learning.[51]

When their relationship was still new, young Frederick often heard Auld read the Bible aloud while her husband wasn't at home. One day, after Frederick had fallen asleep under a table where Auld kept her Bible, he awoke to the sound of her "mellow, loud and sweet" voice reading a lament from the book of Job. Her reading touched him so deeply that the next day he asked her to teach him to read it. By the time he could spell words of three or four letters, Auld was so proud of his learning to read the Bible that she shared his progress with her husband. Douglass later wrote, "Here arose the first cloud over my Baltimore prospects, the precursor of drenching rains and chilling blasts." Hugh Auld rebuked his wife for the mistake of teaching a slave to read because "it would forever unfit him for the duties of a slave." It was the "first decidedly anti-slavery lecture to which it had been my lot to listen."

---

[50] Douglass, *F. D. Papers*. Series two, Autobiographical Writings, vol. 2, 88.
[51] Fought, *Women*, 32–33.

While the rant gave young Frederick a clear sense of his path to freedom, the effect it had on Sophia Auld was awful. This once kind and loving woman became harsh and vigilant in preventing him from reading. "Nature had made us *friends*; slavery made us *enemies*."⁵²

Determined to read at any cost, young Frederick carried a used copy of Noah Webster's spelling book with him and taught himself to read and write whenever he could. He'd ask young white playmates to step aside and give him a lesson, paying them with bread or a biscuit. In *My Bondage,* he wrote, "For a single biscuit, any of my hungry little comrades would give me a lesson more valuable to me than bread." With the younger boys he could say, "I wish I could be free, as you will be when you get to be men." Or, "You will be free, you know, as soon as you are twenty-one, and can go where you like, but I am a slave for life. Have I not as good a right to be free as you have?" Younger boys always agreed he had as good a right as they did.⁵³

Young Frederick began to ask white boys how to spell words or what their meaning was. And, while out and about, he secretly earned small change by blacking boots and put those earnings toward buying his first book.⁵⁴ While Tommy was in school, Frederick, now eleven, did simple tasks at the shipyard like running errands, beating and spinning old ropes called oakum, and turning the grindstone on which tools were sharpened. When others took their dinner break, his job was to keep a fire lit under the steam box of the pitch boiler. While they were away, he practiced his letters with a stick in the dirt or with a bit of chalk, making sure no one saw him.⁵⁵

For Frederick's work on the waterfront, Hugh Auld gave him a few pennies (a penny equaled $2.96 in 2022) every week to buy candy, from which he saved fifty cents ($15 in 2022) toward a copy of *The Columbian Orator,* a collection of essays, poems, and other printed material, that he

---

⁵² Douglass, *Autobiographies,* 216–18, and 228; and 1050; and Preston, *Young F. D.,* 93.
⁵³ Douglass, *Autobiographies,* 223–24.
⁵⁴ Howard W. Coles, *The Cradle of Freedom: A History of the Negro in Rochester, Western New York and Canada, vol. 1* (Rochester, NY: Oxford Press, 1941), 106.
⁵⁵ Douglass, *F. D. Papers.* Series two, Autobiographical Writings, vol. 2. *My Bondage and My Freedom* (New Haven: Yale University Press), 97; and Preston, *Young F. D.,* 95.

bought from Knights bookstore on Thames Street.[56] The more he read and learned, the more frustrated he was over his lot in life. "I was no longer the light-hearted, gleesome boy, full of mirth and play, as when I landed first at Baltimore."[57]

---

[56] Douglass, *F. D. Papers. My Bondage*, 90; McFeely, *F. D.*, 34; Burchard, *F. Douglass*, 39; and U.S. Inflation Calculator for 1830.

[57] Douglass, *F. D. Papers. My Bondage*, 91.

CHAPTER 10

Cast His Cares

Despairing that he might be a slave for the rest of his life, young Frederick searched for God and found relief in the preaching of a white Methodist minister and then a black lay preacher, who both encouraged him to cast his cares on God. Frederick experienced a conversion and, for a time, the glow of his new faith softened the view of his harsh surroundings and increased his desire to study the Bible. Charles Lawson, a black drayman or driver, who prayed three times a day and all day long while he worked, became Frederick's close mentor. Later Douglass recalled gathering pages of the Bible from filthy gutters, washing and drying them, and studying them when he had a chance. Despite Hugh Auld's threats of a whipping, Frederick went to Lawson's house as often as possible and considered him a spiritual father, calling him "Uncle." Between 1831 and 1832, Frederick joined Bethel African Methodist Episcopal Church on Strawberry Alley, studied the Bible with Lawson, and prayed that God would deliver him from bondage.[58]

Frederick read the Bible aloud for hours in the drayman's shack on Happy Alley. "I could teach him 'the letter,' but he could teach me 'the spirit,' and refreshing times we had together. . . ." The old man and the lanky boy went to prayer meetings and Sunday services where Frederick soaked up gospel-shouting sermons. Lawson had a vision in which he saw that Frederick was destined to do great work for the Lord.[59] Although Hugh Auld was aware of Frederick's spend-

---

[58] Preston, *Young F. D.*, 97–98; and Douglass, *Autobiographies*, 231–33, and 1051.
[59] Douglass, *Autobiographies*, 232; and Preston, *Young F. D.*, 97–98.

ing so much time with Lawson, to Auld's credit, he never followed through on his threat of a whipping.[60]

In addition to faith, the other influence on Frederick was *The Columbian Orator* with its inspiring selections on freedom, democracy, and courage. Learning the meaning of the word *abolition,* coupled with freedom, gave him hope for a new life beyond slavery. He diligently practiced his penmanship and began writing for runaways.[61]

---

[60] Douglass, *Autobiographies,* 235.
[61] Douglass, *Narrative,* 109 (note 25).

CHAPTER 11

Economic Slump

No one in the Bailey family had ever been sold to the Deep South when Frederick was born in 1818. But by 1832, the economy on the Eastern Shore had soured. Industries like shipbuilding slowed and wheat growing didn't use as much labor as other crops, and then only in midsummer during harvest time. To his growing horror, Frederick learned what "sold down to Georgia" meant when a sister, two aunts, seven cousins, and five other relatives disappeared.[62] During Frederick's childhood, fifteen members of the Bailey family were sold to southern Cotton States.[63]

As the economic slump hurt Hugh Auld's work as a ship's carpenter, he drank more, and since he and his wife Sophia had two more children to feed and clothe, tensions at home grew. More than Frederick and Sophia having grown distant, Thomas Auld resented having meager service from Henny, whose hands were crippled, while Hugh Auld had the benefit of Frederick's full service. Thomas Auld sent Henny to Baltimore. When Hugh shipped her back, Thomas, as lawful owner of both, insisted that Frederick return, as well.[64]

By the time he was fifteen, Frederick Bailey was larger, older, and wiser than others his age. Although Hugh Auld could have punished him for having books and reading, he didn't. Instead, he sent him to Thomas in St. Michaels from which it was much harder to escape than from Baltimore.[65]

---

[62] Preston, *Young F. D.*, 76.
[63] Douglass, *Autobiographies*, 1051.
[64] Preston, *Young F. D.*, 104.
[65] McFeely, *F. D.*, 39; and Preston, *Young F. D.*, 104–05.

When Frederick returned in March to Thomas Auld's household in St. Michaels, there were eight Aulds living there. Two years after the death of his first wife Lucretia, Thomas married a sickly woman named Rowena. They lived in the house behind Thomas's store, while Frederick, his sister Eliza, their aunt, and a cousin lived in a kitchen building. It was here that Frederick learned that his sister, Sarah, had been sold to a Mississippi planter in 1832.

Rowena Auld and Frederick disliked each other from the start. Rowena, who was twenty-one, was so stingy she locked her well-stocked larder and gave the four slaves about a half peck of cornmeal a week. She would rather have food spoil than give it to them. It was Frederick's sister, Eliza, who taught him to purposely forget Rowena's rules and orders and that it wasn't a sin for them to steal food.[66]

Douglass wrote in *My Bondage* that it was in St. Michaels that a "pious young man," who had heard that Frederick could read and write, invited him to help at a Sabbath school in the house of a free colored man. That young man and Frederick used old spellers and Bible writings to share with what he called their young "scholars." Their first meeting went so well that Frederick felt happy all week waiting for the next one. But church leaders broke up the second meeting. Three leaders of the Methodist Sabbath School, including Thomas Auld, beat them with sticks. Frederick felt betrayed by Thomas Auld and, from then on, the contrast between the Methodists' preaching and practices stung Frederick deeply, and hypocrisy became a lifelong thorn.[67]

A law dating from 1723 gave local constables the right to break up slave meetings on the Sabbath and other holy days, with whatever force necessary, including thirty-nine lashes. Actually, Preston wrote, there was no written law to this effect, but slave meetings were against local customs which allowed workers to read the Bible under the supervision of a responsible white person. Frederick wouldn't have known there was no law in Maryland that kept a master from teaching his slaves to read.[68]

---

[66] Preston, *Young F. D.*, 106–08; and Douglass, *Autobiographies*, 246 and 1051.
[67] Douglass, *Autobiographies*, 254; McFeely, *F. D.*, 43; and Preston, *Young F. D.*, 115–16.
[68] Preston, *Young F. D.*, 14 and 216 (note 47).

Years later when his master denied ever having struck him or telling anyone to do so, Douglass recalled a time, most likely over the summer of 1833, when Thomas Auld had accused Frederick of knowing where a missing carriage lamp was and beat Frederick until Auld exhausted himself. Recalling how Auld used to beat others, Douglass also wrote of times between 1838 and 1840 when he had seen Auld whip his crippled cousin Henny Bailey. After Thomas Auld inherited her in 1826, he tied her up in the morning, quoted Scriptures as he beat her, left her there, and beat her again in the evening. Auld sent Henny to his sister, who sent her back, at which point Auld set Henny loose to fend for herself. Douglass later wrote, "Bad as my condition was when I lived with Master Thomas, I was soon to experience a life far more goading and bitter."[69]

---

[69] Douglass, *Autobiographies,* 255; and Preston, *Young F. D,* 111 and 113.

CHAPTER 12

Farm Work

Because Frederick had lived in the city, Thomas Auld said Frederick was unsuited to work on the Auld farm. Starting in January 1834, Frederick was sent to Edward Covey's farm where, he shivered through cold nights in an unheated attic. Despite being religious, Covey was a hardworking, bullish farmer, who crept and crawled in the grass to spy on his slaves. Among themselves, the slaves called Covey "the snake." Covey overworked his slaves in cold and hot weather, and whipped or beat Frederick weekly.

One time, on a sweltering day in August when Frederick grew weak, Covey kicked him to make him work, and accused him of faking his condition. Frederick fled to Thomas Auld for safety, but Auld told him to go back to Covey. Frederick took his time, resting and eating before going back. Covey, angry at Frederick's insubordination, planned to tie him up and beat him. But when the time came, Frederick fought back. They struggled fiercely with neither overcoming the other. That was the last lashing Covey ever gave the young man.[70] Booker T. Washington wrote, "To the other slaves he became a hero, and Covey was not anxious to advertise his complete failure to break in this 'unruly nigger.' It speaks well for the natural dignity and good sense of young Douglass that he neither boasted of his triumph, nor did anything rash as a consequence of it, as might have been expected from a boy of his age and spirit." On Christmas Day, 1834, Frederick's work year was done, and he learned he was to be sent elsewhere.[71]

---

[70] Douglass, *Autobiographies*, 255, 258, 265, 275, 281, and 284–285.

[71] Booker T. Washington, *Frederick Douglass* (Philadelphia: George W. Jacobs and Co., 1906), 41.

In the meantime, Colonel Lloyd had died in June 1834, and his estate included twenty-one outlying farms of about 9,000, each run by an overseer who was paid $120 ($4,135 in 2022) to $135 ($4,651 in 2022) a year. Each farm had eighteen to almost fifty slaves, including the young and the elderly. When Douglass visited the estate as an older man, he remembered Lloyd as "a gentleman of the olden time, elegant in his apparel, dignified in his deportment, a man of few words and of weighty presence. . . . No governor of the State of Maryland ever commanded a larger measure of respect."[72]

During the week between Christmas and New Year's, when Frederick returned to Thomas Auld's home, Frederick saw how the slaves' drinking until the New Year, kept them so drunk they were relieved to get back to work in the fields. This made a lasting impression on Douglass. He saw that this deliberate practice of distracting the slaves with liquor during the holidays, kept them too drunk to rebel and removed the slaveholders' fear of their acting up.[73]

The brutal year on Covey's farm turned Frederick Bailey into a first-rate field hand. Starting January 1, 1835, Thomas Auld then placed him with a more lenient master, William Freeland, who didn't whip or starve his slaves, attend a church, or expect his slaves to go to church either. Instead, Frederick worked from sunrise to sunset under Freeland, who gave his workers enough food and even allowed them enough time to eat it.[74]

"As summer came on and the long Sabbath days stretched themselves over our idleness, I became uneasy and wanted a Sabbath school." After the scene when the first Sabbath School at St. Michaels was broken up, they were all aware that, "We might have met to drink whiskey, to wrestle, fight and to do other unseemly things with no fear of interruption."[75]

Washington wrote, "With these new and better conditions and with these superior companions in bondage, Douglass felt a renewal of that old impulse to do something for his fellow slaves. He naturally first turned to the thought

---

[72] Preston, *Young F.D.*, 48, and 49, note 16.
[73] Douglass, *Autobiographies*, 292; and McFeely, *F. D.*, 49.
[74] Douglass, *Autobiographies*, 297; and Preston, *Young F. D.*, 129–30.
[75] Douglass, *Autobiographies*, 298–99.

of teaching them to read and write. He found time and spirit again to look at his library,—the blue-back speller and the *Columbian Orator*. He first started a Sunday-school under the trees, at a safe distance from the "big house," gathering together some thirty young people. They were making fine progress, when, one Sunday, his former experience was repeated, and they were rushed upon and scattered. The school was again started, however, and this time Douglass seems successfully to have evaded the vigilance of his master. In addition to the Sunday-school, he devoted three evenings a week to his fellow slaves."[76]

According to author David Blight, Douglass later wrote, "The fact is, here I began my public speaking." As for the various types of work he had done over the years, he wrote, "I look back to none with more satisfaction than to that afforded by my Sunday school."[77]

"Having satisfied himself that his companions were proof against treachery and were of the right sort of mettle, he began to study the practical means of escape," Washington wrote. "There were no well-marked routes from slavery to freedom, no highways, byways, or 'underground railways,' known to him at that time. Such knowledge belonged wholly to the region north of the boundary line of freedom. He had heard of slaves escaping, but how they got away and by what route was always a mystery. He had heard that there was a region called North, and that in this far haven, white and black people alike were free. He had heard of a land called Canada, but its location on maps and charts was unknown to him."[78]

Frederick had decided at the beginning of 1836 to achieve his freedom within the year. On April 2, he and six others stole the log oyster-gathering canoe of a prosperous farmer—that Douglass described as a "large canoe"—to travel along the Eastern Shore to a canal near North Point where they could slip into Pennsylvania. They were all caught. The others were returned to their farms, but Frederick was locked in the local jail. "After remaining in this life of misery and despair about a week, which by the way, seemed a month, Master

---

[76] Washington, *F. Douglass*, 41–42.
[77] Blight, *F. D. Prophet*, 68–9.
[78] Washington, *F. Douglass*, 44.

Thomas . . . came to the prison, and took me out, for the purpose, as he said, of sending me to Alabama, with a friend of his, who would emancipate me at the end of eight years." Frederick had no faith that that man would ever free him and since he had never heard of this friend in Alabama, he took it as a convenient story to ship him to the Deep South.[79]

Washington wrote, "While in this condition of dejection and hopelessness, the unexpected happened. His owner, Thomas Auld, who, in spite of Douglass's rebelliousness, always cherished a peculiar fondness for him, ordered his release from jail, and at once decided to send him back to Baltimore to live with Mr. and Mrs. Hugh Auld. In telling Fred what he intended to do, he said that he wanted him to learn a trade, and that if he would behave himself and give him no more trouble, he would emancipate him when he became twenty-five years old. . . . The good-heartedness of Thomas Auld was the only thing that preserved our young hero for that larger life which he was to make for himself, and help to make for so many others of his race."[80]

---

[79] McFeely, *F. D.*, 36 and 51; Douglass, *Autobiographies*, 303, 308, 313 and 323–325; and Preston, *Young F. D.*, 134 and 136.

[80] Washington, *F. Douglass*, 42.

CHAPTER 13

Apprenticeship

"Hugh Auld easily succeeded in getting young Douglass apprenticed to a caulker in the large ship-yards of William Gardiner, on Fell's Point," Washington explained. "The conditions under which he had to work were very trying; he did not mind the severe labor, but he was much disturbed by the intense prejudice existing among the white boys and mechanics. During the six months that he worked with this firm, everyone seemed to have license to make use of and abuse him. He was not a coward, and would quickly strike back at a man who insulted or attempted to maltreat him. Finally, however, he was assaulted by a crowd of ruffians and frightfully beaten. His face was swollen and he was covered with blood. In this condition, he reported himself to Mr. Auld, who was furious when he beheld the pitiable state of his slave. Mrs. Auld took pity upon him and kindly dressed his wounds, and nursed him until they were healed. In the meantime he was angrily withdrawn from Mr. Gardiner's employ, and it was sought to bring to punishment the perpetrators of the assault."[81]

Frederick's job, at the beck and call of seventy-five carpenters who worked on two warships ended, after four white apprentices beat him so badly that he almost lost his left eye. Unlike Thomas Auld who had sided with Covey's beatings, Hugh Auld stood up for Frederick in court, but without success, since none of the fifty white witnesses would testify on Frederick's behalf.

Hugh Auld then hired out Frederick as a caulking apprentice in another yard where Auld was foreman. Frederick became so skilled that, within a year, he could hire out himself at the highest wage paid for experienced caulkers.

---

[81] Washington, *F. Douglass*, 51.

He found that more freedom increased his desire for total freedom. Although Frederick couldn't have helped noticing that three of the fast-sailing ships they worked on were intended for the slave trade, he wouldn't have known that Congress had outlawed the slave trade as piracy in 1820. The profits were so great that this law was ignored in Southern states.[82]

Washington wrote that Frederick "soon found that the difficulties of escape were quite as great in Baltimore as on the Freeland plantation. The railroads running from that city to Philadelphia were compelled to enforce the most stringent regulations with reference to colored people. Even free Negroes found it difficult to comply with them. Every one applying for a railway ticket was required to show his 'free papers' and to be measured and carefully examined before he could enter the cars. Besides this, he was not allowed to travel by night. Similar regulations were enforced by steamboat companies. In addition to all these difficulties, every road and turnpike was picketed with kidnappers on the lookout for fugitive slaves. Douglass found it much easier to learn the obstacles than the aids to successful escape."[83]

---

[82] Douglass, *Autobiographies*, 328–329 and 336; and Burchard, *F. Douglass*, 67.
[83] Washington, *F. Douglass*, 54–55.

CHAPTER 14

Betterment

In 1836, at the age of eighteen, when Frederick returned to Baltimore, he could no longer accept the attitude of the lay leaders at Bethel African Methodist Episcopal Church because of their stand against abolitionist zealots like William Lloyd Garrison and his American Anti-Slavery Society. Instead, Frederick joined Sharp Street AME Church, which was more moderate about abolition of slavery.[84]

"There was at that time an organization of free colored people, known as the East Baltimore [Mental] Improvement Society," Washington wrote. "Although membership in this exclusive body was limited to free people, young Douglass was eagerly admitted. This was the first organization of any kind, outside of the church, to which he had ever belonged. It is probable that he had here his first opportunity to exercise his natural gift of eloquence."[85] Frederick later remembered the young men and caulkers in the society who knew how to "read, write and cipher" and had "high notions about mental improvement."[86]

Frederick became close to five of the young men in the Improvement Society, who he thought were gifted and would have had great chances for success had they received the same treatment as young white men. He became their intellectual leader. One evening, after mimicking the hypocritical style of white ministers preaching about love and freedom while ignoring slaves' deep longing for "the joys of liberty," he announced his intention to be a United States

---

[84] Preston, *Young F. D.*, 149–150.

[85] Washington, *F. Douglass*, 52.

[86] Fought, *Women*, 47.

senator. "Fred Bailey's speaking career began first on Freeland's farm and then in Happy Alley in Baltimore," Preston wrote.

A friend from that time later wrote to Douglass that the East Baltimore Mental Improvement Society met in Happy Alley. Historians disagree as to whether the group had gatherings at which Frederick could have met Anna Murray. Since Fell's Point was a close-knit neighborhood, Murray could have met him at the market, Strawberry Alley Church, or friends' homes. The minister at her funeral said she had first met him at church. Fought claimed that the Improvement Society had a men-only membership with no formal social events and that most women avoided public activities that weren't centered on charities. Fought referred to a letter that Frederick received in 1870 about the Society that mentioned Murray's remembering some of the names of men in the group. According to Fought, Frederick also remembered those young men.[87]

---

[87] Preston, *Young F. D.*, 148–49; Fought, *Women*, 47; and Blight, *F. D. Prophet*, 78–79.

CHAPTER 15

The Murray Family

Anna Murray's parents, Mary and Bambarra Murray, were slaves who lived on Maryland's Eastern Shore near the town of Denton in Caroline County on the west side of Tuckahoe Creek. That region, called Tuckahoe Neck, was about three miles from the section of Tuckahoe Creek where Frederick Bailey had been born. The Murrays had twelve children, seven born into slavery and five born free. Murray later told her children that her mother had been set free a month before Anna's birth, without explaining the details. Anna was their first child to be born free.

Murray, her sisters, Elizabeth and Charlotte, and her brother, Philip, moved to Baltimore about 1830 or 1831 to find a better life than was possible in a rural area. It's probable that the Mary Murray listed as running a shop that sold cooked food on Ruxton Street in Baltimore in 1836 was Anna's mother. Running a cookshop was one way for women to advance themselves.[88]

At age seventeen, Anna Murray started to work for two years for Francis and Elizabeth Montell, a French Creole family from the Bahamas that had moved to Pratt Street in Baltimore with their eight children. Francis Montell had been a merchant in the West Indies, who had had twenty-five slaves until he sold them in 1832 and moved, possibly because of talk of emancipation—the releasing of all enslaved people—which occurred in the British West Indies on August 1, 1834. In Baltimore, Montell and his son owned a shop on the Inner Harbor, a close-knit neighborhood where the *Sally Lloyd* would have docked.[89]

---

[88] McFeely, *F. D.*, 67; Blight, *F. D. Prophet*, 79; and Fought, *Women*, 41–42.
[89] Fought, *Women*, 43, and 83.

After Murray left the Montells, she worked in the home of Mr. Wells, Baltimore's postmaster, where she earned her reputation as a highly skilled housekeeper. The Wells family lived on Caroline Street, a few blocks from the Montells. Murray stayed with the Wellses for several years and kept fond memories of her years with the Montell family. Earlier in his life, Peter Wells had lived on Aliceanna Street where Frederick once lived with Hugh and Sophia Auld. After working for the post office in the 1820s and 30s, Wells and his family eventually moved to Caroline Street. In those days, families with hired help considered themselves middle class. By working for both the Montells and the Wellses, Murray was well trained in middle-class ways.[90]

Before then, Anna Murray's mother would have trained her to cook and clean so she could find steady work and possibly the mistress of the house in both places would have done chores with Murray while giving her instructions, Fought wrote. Murray would have already learned all the steps needed for gathering, storing, and preparing foods from when she lived with her family in Caroline County. But, now, shopping on her own or with her mistress in Baltimore, she would have bought butter, cut meats, fresh-picked produce, and candles.

Standards of cleanliness in the nineteenth century were different from those of today. Between all kinds of mud, filth, and dust outdoors, and dust from open hearths indoors, it was very difficult to keep homes spotless. It took Murray several years to learn the middle-class habits of keeping a dust-free home and always being neatly dressed, compared to the lifestyle and work clothes she grew up with in the country. Murray raised herself above the mean-spirited stereotypes of working-class and poor black women. Her skills as well as smart appearance reflected favorably on her employers and made her a desirable employee. It isn't possible to say how easily she got along with her employers. Having grown up in a slave society, she seems to have deliberately worked her way out of the lower ranks into which her family had been born. In bettering herself, Murray developed the reserve that was proper for a person of her race, class, and work status. Her training in Baltimore gave her, what a later neighbor in Rochester, New

---

[90] Blight, *F. D. Prophet*, 79; Rosetta Sprague, "My Mother As I Recall Her," paper given at Women's Christian Temperance Union, May 10, 1900, 6; and Fought, *Women*, 43–44.

York, called "aristocratic ideas," and that neighbor guessed that she had worked for Southern families "of high standing." Just as her future husband had learned to read from Tommy Auld's mother and others around him, Murray learned in Baltimore the skills that made her "the banker" of her family after they moved North.[91] Murray usually wore a plain white or gray calico dress, an apron, and a head scarf. Blight thought she may have worn a nicer dress or scarf on the day she met Frederick.[92]

Murray had already learned to play the violin and introduced Frederick to it. According to Burchard he had a good singing voice, and they enjoyed singing together, becoming so caught up in learning new songs that they acquired a large collection of sheet music. Their love grew and they decided to marry.[93] Preston wrote, "With Anna's encouragement [Frederick] took up music, starting a lifelong love affair with the violin; together they bought three volumes of collected musical pieces . . . which would be cherished possessions for many years."[94] McFeely wrote that Frederick received encouragement from Murray, who worked in the Wells home. He could have learned to play the violin from someone at the E. M. P. Wells School that Mrs. Elizabeth Wells ran on Caroline Street, and with practice, Frederick became a competent amateur violinist. With his skill of mimicry, Frederick could have learned the basics, but he had to have talent to play Mozart as well as he did.[95]

Anna Murray had several decisions to make. As a free black woman who lived with her employers, she might not have had the option to live with her husband. Also, as a free black woman married to a slave, their life together was threatened by the possibility of his being sold and sent elsewhere. Not only would she have to work in others' homes, but Murray would also have to do all her own housework as well. As for Frederick, he would face highs and lows

---

[91] Fought, *Women*, 44–45.
[92] Blight, *F. D. Prophet*, 79.
[93] Burchard, *F. Douglass*, 69.
[94] Preston, *Young F. D.*, 151–152 and 229, (note 16).
[95] McFeely, *F. D.*, 17, and 65–66.

finding jobs, depending on his line of work. According to Fought, these challenges were the norm for a woman of her station in life.[96]

Murray had the same sense of self-reliance and loyalty that Frederick's grandmother and mother, Betsey and Harriet Bailey, had. As with other women he became close to as an adult—Julia Griffiths, Ottilie Assing, and Helen Pitts—Murray didn't fit the Victorian model of a meek child-wife. Yet, Diedrich didn't include Murray as a competent woman who could teach him the social skills that few black women had in those days, and that these middle-class white women could.[97]

A traditional marriage wasn't an option for Frederick and Anna in Baltimore. It was an option only for whites and few blacks, Fought wrote. Romantic love was less important than whether each person balanced the demands of a household and family. Their marriage fit the norm for black and working-class marriages. Her skills as a competent housekeeper paired with his skills as a caulker with a high-paying job, were a good fit. Unlike many of their peers who were often in debt, they knew how to save.[98]

---

[96] Fought, *Women*, 46.
[97] Maria Diedrich, *Love Across Color Lines* (New York: Hill and Wang, 1999), 171–72.
[98] Fought, *Women*, 49–50.

CHAPTER 16

Plans for Escape

Meanwhile, in early spring 1838, Thomas Auld, who was in Baltimore on business, had refused Frederick's request to be allowed to hire himself out and live on his own. Then, in May of that year, Frederick convinced Hugh Auld to allow him to turn over his wages weekly to Auld. Frederick kept his word for a time, but broke his word in August, when he stayed through the weekend at an outdoor religious camp meeting and didn't pay up until Monday. Auld was furious. On August 12, Frederick made the decision to flee on September 3. He had three weeks to come up with a plan. Decades later, Douglass told historian Wilbur. H. Siebert that, because he had helped other runaways plan their escapes, he was familiar with the close ties between the AME churches in Baltimore and Philadelphia and didn't rely on chance.[99]

One of the jobs Frederick had taken to earn extra money when he was living on his own was that of a servant, calling himself Edward. According to McFeely, it's possible that, as a handsome, light-skinned young man, he easily found work as a butler in the home of John Merryman, a stockbroker. One of Frederick's duties was to walk a son of Mr. Merriman (or Merryman) from his house on Calvert Street to the E. M. P. Wells School. Mrs. Elizabeth Wells's school on Caroline Street was close to where Anna Murray stayed. There's a chance Frederick and Anna met around the Fell's Point neighborhood or that Murray referred him for the position. According to Fought, Frederick's experience caring for children might have helped him get that job.[100]

---

[99] McFeely, *F. D.*, 70; and Preston, *Young F. D.*, 151, and 153.
[100] Fought, *Women*, 48; and McFeely, *F. D.*, 65.

Between May and August, Frederick worked diligently, bought his own tools, and also used his free time, perhaps at Murray's suggestion, to take up music at church.[101]

After having to move back with Hugh Auld's family, Frederick worked as a caulker, put in two full weeks and earned $18 ($624 in 2022), which he gave to Auld, who gave him back $.25 ($8 in 2022). The third week, he worked four days, and gave Auld $6 ($208 in 2022). Frederick saved $17 ($589 in 2022), which was not enough to cover a train ticket and travel costs. Murray sold one of her two featherbeds and used her savings to make ends meet. He wrote, "How I got away in what direction I traveled whether by land or by water; whether without or without assistance—must for reasons already mentioned, remain unexplained."[102]

---

[101] Blight, *F. D. Prophet*, 80.

[102] Douglass, *Autobiographies,* 347, Preston, *Young F. D.*153-54; and U.S. Inflation Calculator for 1838.

CHAPTER 17

An Abolitionist's Life

Frederick Bailey endured a nerve-wracking trip by train, ferry, another train, and a steamboat to Philadelphia where a black porter directed him to the right ferry. He then took a night train and another ferry to New York City and arrived exhausted but thrilled by his new freedom. By chance, he met a black whitewasher he had known in Baltimore, who had since changed his name. That man warned Frederick to trust no one and avoid colored boarding houses that slave catchers monitored. Fearful of getting caught, that night he slept hungry and tired, behind some barrels. He knew he was supposed to go to David Ruggle's house, but was unwilling to ask for help. The next day, he met a sailor who took him in for the night and delivered him safely to Ruggles's home nearby. Ruggles, director of the New York Committee of Vigilance, was described as "the remarkable, stalwart friend of all runaways."[103]

David Ruggles edited the *Mirror of Liberty*, the first black-owned and black-run magazine in the United States, which included reports of the Vigilance Committee's activities helping runaways. Ruggles also had a public reading room in his home filled with books and newspapers supporting abolition. He was in and out of court for his activities, and it was at Ruggles's home that Frederick saw what the daily life of abolitionists looked like.[104] Ruggles persuaded Frederick to look for work as a caulker in New Bedford, Massachusetts. Heeding the advice not to trust anyone and trying to make it

---

[103] McFeely, *F. D.*, 71–73.
[104] Blight, *F. D. Prophet*, 84 (footnote 33).

difficult for slave hunters to find him, Frederick Bailey changed his name to Frederick Johnson.[105]

Frederick wrote to Anna, who joined him in New York, bringing a feather bed, pillows, bed linens, dishes, knives, forks and spoons, and a trunk full of clothes, including a new plum silk dress for the wedding. They were married on September 15, 1838 by the Rev. James W. C. Pennington, who had been a slave and blacksmith on Maryland's Eastern Shore.[106]

In the beginning of his 1845 autobiography, *Narrative of the Life of a Slave*, Douglass wrote of his undocumented birth and the rapes and beating of slave women. He ended *Narrative* with details about his marriage, the certificate, the witnesses, and the name of a legitimate minister. While slaves didn't usually have last names, Frederick and Anna took "Johnson" as their new last name in New York State, and Frederick was deliberate about showing the legitimacy of their marriage. Once they had their marriage certificate, David Ruggles gave Frederick $5 ($159 in 2022) and a letter of introduction to a contact in Newport, Rhode Island, which was a stop on their way to New Bedford. Frederick and Anna boarded a steamboat and were so eager to finish the trip, they decided not to stay in Newport. From Newport, they took a stage coach to their final destination and, since they didn't have the fare, promised to pay it upon their arrival.[107]

---

[105] Douglass, *Autobiographies*, 91.

[106] Sprague, "My Mother", 9; and Douglass, *F. D. Papers*. Series three, Correspondence, vol. 1, 27 (note 3).

[107] Fought, *Women*, 51–52; Douglass, *F. D. Papers*. Series two, Autobiographical Writings, vol. 1, 76; and U.S. Inflation Calculator for 1838.

CHAPTER 18

New Bedford, Massachusetts

In 1838, New Bedford's 12,000 inhabitants included about 300 escapees, living among about 1,000 free blacks. Its port was home to about 170 ships in the whaling industry that employed 4,000 workers. Those young workers included eccentrics of all types from rural New England and countries across distant oceans.[108]

In the 1830s, New Bedford, in Bristol County, Massachusetts, was a port city that had become wealthy from whaling and shipbuilding. It had a population that grew from about 7,500 at the beginning of the 1830s to nearly 12,000 by the end of the decade. New Bedford had a strong anti-slavery stance in the black community which had private schools, a Christian society, and an African Methodist Episcopal Zion church. There were boarding houses run by black men for black mariners, and craftsmen, such as blacksmiths, who offered connections to David Ruggles in New York City. This community helped escaped slaves and their families adapt to life in the North. Despite the absence of slavery, segregation on transportation, and in churches, schools, and the courts was common, and socializing across the color line wasn't permitted.

Yet, gradually, black church members and white Quakers met in growing numbers in integrated anti-slavery societies. When Frederick and Anna Johnson moved to New Bedford, they fit into a community that matched what they had

---

[108] Blight, *F. D. Prophet*, 89.

left behind in Baltimore. Even though they mourned losing touch with family in the South, they found comfort with others in their same situation.[109]

After the newlyweds reached New Bedford, they roomed with a black couple, Mary and Nathan Johnson. She had a confectionery shop in part of the house, and he was the leading caterer in New Bedford—the richest city, per capita, in the United States. Nathan, who was described as a sociable man, was listed as "c. confectionary" in the city directory. He was the only black member of the library society, which allowed him to use its reading room but not to attend events in its lecture hall.

Despite Mary and Nathan Johnson's house having once been a Friends' meetinghouse, New Bedford's Quaker meetings weren't integrated. Even so, the Quakers were committed to ending slavery, and Massachusetts was more welcoming to blacks than Rhode Island. As part of introducing them to life in the North, Nathan recommended that Frederick choose a different surname because there was a full page of Johnsons in the city directory. Nathan suggested "Douglas" and Frederick chose to spell it with two s's. After being told he couldn't compete with white men for skilled work as a caulker, he borrowed tools from Nathan to chop wood. He also did heavy lifting, shoveled, dug, cleared, scoured, loaded, and unloaded vessels.[110]

Even though Frederick and Anna must have considered what their married life in Baltimore would have been like with his having a good-paying job and her working as a live-in domestic, they had left to face a new life in an unknown place. For their first few months in New Bedford, they lived apart while she worked as a live-in maid. She quit that winter when she became pregnant, which was typical for the time—pregnant women didn't work as live-in domestics. She and Frederick moved out of the second floor of the Johnson's home to two rooms in a house on Elm Street. Anna began taking in laundry. Over the winter months, Frederick had no seasonal work as a day laborer, but

---

[109] Fought, *Women*, 52, 53, and 55.
[110] McFeely, *F. D.*, 76, 78, and 79.

in the spring, he found a steady job moving casks of whale oil—hard work that required strength and stamina.[111]

"Up to this time [Douglass] had known but two classes of white people, slave-holders and nonslave-holders," Washington wrote. "The non-slave holding white people of the South, he knew, were generally ignorant, despised, and poor; while those who owned slaves seemed to own everything else worth having. Here in New England he observed that white people were high or low according to their character, ability, and possessions. Life appeared to him larger, wider, and fuller of possibilities than he had dreamed, even in his more hopeful days down on the Eastern Shore. . . . He was liked by everybody who employed him, because he made it a matter of principle to do all and more than his full duty in every occupation. He put as much zeal, intelligence, and cheerful industry into these common tasks as he later gave to pursuits of a more dignified character.

"Young Douglass," Washington continued, "was cheered and heartened in this wholesome atmosphere of freedom,—free schools, free labor, and general fair play, to such a degree that it was a long time before he began to feel the presence and trammels of race prejudice as they existed in New Bedford and elsewhere in the North in that day. That there was a feeling against his color he learned when he attempted to follow his trade as a caulker."[112]

Douglass was also stunned at one white church service in which the minister called white people from the main pews forward for communion and then, in a high-pitched voice, called black worshipers "black sheep" from the gallery to the altar rail. Frederick walked out.[113]

---

[111] Fought, *Women*, 55–56.

[112] Washington, *F. Douglass*, 64–65.

[113] Blight, *F. D. Prophet*, 92–3, and 94.

CHAPTER 19

A New Community

A few months after arriving in New Bedford, Douglass was offered a trial subscription to a weekly abolitionist paper called *The Liberator*, which he soon prized. During his first three years in New Bedford, he worked at any job he could find and learned as much as he could about the anti-slavery cause. "*The Liberator* was a paper after my own heart. It detested slavery—exposed hypocrisy and wickedness in high places—made no truce with the traffickers in the bodies and souls of men. . . Every week the *Liberator* came, and every week I made myself master of its contents."[114]

William Lloyd Garrison, editor of *The Liberator*, was already harshly criticized for his stand against slavery and in favor of unconditional immediate emancipation. The first issue of *The Liberator* was published in January 1, 1831. By the end of that year, the State of Georgia offered a $5,000 reward ($161,579 in 2022) for Garrison's kidnapping.[115]

When Douglass first read *The Liberator*, he learned that anti-slavery activism existed all across the North; that immediatism demanded no concessions to anything that endorsed slavery in churches, government, or community life. He learned of massive campaigns to persuade Congress to end slavery in the District of Columbia and the western territories, and of the gag rules used to silence the few anti-slavery members of Congress. He read about leading black abolitionists like James McCune Smith, with whom he later had a lasting

---

[114] Douglass, *F. D. Papers*. Series two, Autobiographical Writings, vol. 2, 204, and 205.
[115] Holland, *F. D. Colored Orator*, 45; and U.S. Inflation Calculator for 1831.

friendship.[116] According to Washington, after the setback of not being able to work as a caulker, Douglass "met his next rebuff when he attempted to attend one of the lectures under the auspices of the New Bedford Lyceum Association. He was refused a ticket on the ground that it was against the policy of the society to admit colored people to the lecture room. It was not long, however, before this discrimination was done away with, since men like Charles Sumner, [Ralph Waldo] Emerson, Horace Mann, and Garrison, refused to speak before the organization unless the restriction was removed. The privilege of attending these meetings and hearing some of the great anti-slavery leaders was a matter of great import to Douglass."[117]

Douglass first attended other churches in New Bedford but switched to Zion chapel, an African Methodist Episcopal Zion denomination. It was there that he met Bishop Christopher Rush, who made him an exhorter—a lay person authorized to hold meetings, lead prayers, and preach. Douglass fondly remembered his many roles at "little Zion" where he met a new preacher, the Rev. Thomas James. Ordained by Rush in 1833, Rev. James fused his fervor and zeal to end slavery and licensed Douglass as a lay preacher. Douglass first spoke briefly at a church meeting in 1839 about what slavery was like. A short time later, Rev. James saw Douglass in the audience and invited him to speak. This time Douglass shared his own story. "Little Zion" was where, Douglass later wrote, he had his first chance to "exercise [his] gifts." The encouragement and opportunities to give sermons from the pulpit, launched his new vocation in advocacy.

From reading *The Liberator*, Douglass was introduced to William Lloyd Garrison's radical writings, and also to women's roles in the abolition movement in organizing, fund-raising and recruiting. In April 1839, Douglass heard Garrison speak for the first time and was taken by Garrison's strong and passionate voice.[118]

"The colored people of New Bedford were the first to discover [Douglass's] fluency as a speaker and to give ear to his original ideas on the question of

---

[116] Blight, *F. D. Prophet*, 94–95.

[117] Washington, *F. Douglass*, 66.

[118] Blight, *F. D. Prophet*, 93–97.

freedom for their race," Washington wrote. "He was often called upon to speak in meetings held by colored men in the town, and in colored churches. As far as the masses of the people were concerned, however, he was still an obscure Negro laborer. There was no one except, perhaps, Nathan Johnson, who saw in this patient and cheerful toiler the promise of a public career. No men of African descent had up to this time achieved anything like distinction. . . . But the power within this young fugitive slave and the forces without him were fast shaping themselves to call him forth and hold him up as an example to all the world."[119]

"It was at Methodist prayer meetings that Douglass learned to speak in a way that made people listen and found out he spoke in a way that few others did," wrote Jane Marsh Parker, his neighbor later in Rochester, New York. "He knew the Bible better than most, read it frequently, and later said, 'I am in the trade-winds of God. My bark was launched by Him, and He is taking it into port'."[120]

Over the winter of 1839, Douglass was a regular speaker at AME Zion Church, a small congregation of fugitive slaves and free blacks. He practiced Bible lessons and read Scriptures in front of a supportive congregation. Whether people like him, born in the United States and escaped from slavery, ought to choose to move back to Africa or elsewhere, troubled him enough to take a stand. His first publicly recorded speech was at a meeting on March 12, 1839, where he was one of ten blacks from New Bedford, who spoke up against colonization. They recited the first lines of the Declaration of Independence, called out colonization as tyrannical, and declared themselves American citizens. This may be considered the first public stand in his life-long criticism of colonization. The occasion was described in *The Liberator* later that month.[121] Around the summer of 1840, white abolitionists discovered the young black speaker. In a letter dated August 20, 1840, Boston anti-slavery lawyer Ellis Gray Loring wrote to a friend in Toronto about a colored man Loring was eager to

---

[119] Washington, *F. Douglass*, 67–68.

[120] Jane Marsh Parker, "Reminiscences of Frederick Douglass," in Coles, *Cradle*, Chapter XXXIII, 159.

[121] Blight, *F. D. Prophet*, 97–98.

hire as a speaker. Loring asked his friend to contact Thomas Auld about buying Douglass's freedom, but the attempt failed.[122]

During their first years in New Bedford, Frederick and Anna welcomed two children into the two-room home that looked out on a bay in New Bedford: Rosetta in June, 1839, and Lewis Henry in July, 1840.

By the late 1830s, since black and white men in Massachusetts could register to vote by paying a small annual tax, Douglass paid a $1.50 ($45 in 2022) poll tax to register in either 1839 or 1840. By 1841, the family had moved from their small house into a larger house on Ray Street, where Anna enjoyed having a garden. In the evenings, Frederick played Haydn, Mozart, and Handel on his violin. It was like the life Anna had known in Baltimore. They were expecting another child.[123] The 1841 New Bedford directory listed Douglass's occupation as "Rev." instead of "laborer."[124]

During the time he was speaking at AME Zion church, leading local meetings to oppose colonization and addressing white audiences at the Bristol County Anti-Slavery Society in New Bedford, Douglass also listened to speeches by notable abolitionists, including another former slave from Maryland—the Rev. Henry Highland Garnet. Blight wrote that Douglass remembered Rev. Garnet's speech in May 1841 for a long time as deeply inspiring. One or more speeches that Douglass gave in New Bedford, in turn inspired white bookseller and abolitionist William C. Coffin to invite Douglass to join the Massachusetts Anti-Slavery Society (MASS) for its grand convention on the island of Nantucket.[125]

On August 9, 1841, after prominent white men abolitionists spoke during the day at the Bristol County Anti-Slavery Society meeting in Liberty Hall in New Bedford, colored speakers addressed the group at the evening session. Blight wrote that most likely Douglass was among those who spoke about problems on public transportation and segregated churches. The next day, Frederick and Anna took a steamer to Nantucket, one of the few times Anna went to

---

[122] Blight, *F. D. Prophet*, 93 (footnote 13).

[123] McFeely, *F. D.*, 82; and Douglass, *Autobiographies*, chronology, 1054.

[124] Blight, *F. D. Prophet*, 94.

[125] Blight, *F. D. Prophet*, 98.

one of his speeches. After the captain insisted that about forty black passengers move to the upper deck, white abolitionists joined them in the sun and rain for the trip. About a thousand abolitionists went to the MASS convention where, after Garrison spoke, Douglass was one of five men who stood to support a resolution against discrimination. Douglass spoke briefly before the meeting ended. Accounts from notable leaders implied that the second day of the convention, August 11, was the first time he had ever spoken so intensely about his trials as a slave, and Douglass himself called it his first speech.[126]

Washington wrote, "Douglass went to see, listen, and learn. This was privilege enough for one occasion. When he was sought out by a citizen of New Bedford, who had heard of him, and was asked to say a few words, he was quite startled. So frightened was he, 'it was with much difficulty,' he says, 'that I could stand erect or could command or articulate two words without hesitation and stammering. I trembled in every limb. I am not sure that my embarrassment was not the most important part of my speech, if speech it could be called. The audience sympathized with me and at once, from having been remarkably silent, it became much excited.'

"But his embarrassment soon subsided," Washington continued. "Parker Pillsbury, an eye-witness, says: 'When the young man, Douglass, closed late in the evening, none seemed to know or care for the lateness of the hour. The crowded congregation had been wrought up almost to enchantment as he turned over the terrible apocalypse of his experience in slavery'."[127]

Douglass remembered what he had learned from studying *The Columbian Orator* and for two hours shared a riveting account of his life. It is considered his first great public speech and was followed by Garrison's demanding if it were right that he be held a slave in a Christian land. The white Quakers sprang to their feet and shouted, "No, no. Never, never!"[128] "Measured by its effect on the audience and by its importance to himself and the Abolition cause, this first speech was one of the greatest Mr. Douglass ever made," Washington wrote.

---

[126] Blight, *F. D. Prophet*, 98–99.

[127] Washington, *F. Douglass*, 70–71.

[128] McFeely, *F. D.*, 88–89.

"Only three years out of bondage, never having been at school, wholly self-taught and coming direct from hard toil to a platform, he had been invited to speak before an audience of proud and cultured New Englanders!"[129]

At the age of twenty-two and now the father of two children, Fought wrote that Douglass was used to speaking in front of both men and women because black men and women sat together in church and at informal schools. An integrated anti-slavery meeting presented the problem of mixed gatherings of men and women as well as blacks and whites. Racist attitudes had allowed white slave-owning women to treat him kindly while he was a child. But as an adult, a black man's maleness was considered a threat. From first hearing about something called "abolition" in Baltimore, to moving to New Bedford and reading *The Liberator*, Douglass's ideas about equal rights developed gradually. His speech at the Massachusetts Anti-Slavery Convention in Nantucket in August 1841 was his first before a group of mostly white people which, he admitted later, was something he was not used to and about which he felt "greatly embarrassed."[130]

"Immediately after the convention," Washington wrote, "John A. Collins, then the general agent of the Massachusetts Anti-Slavery Society, went to Mr. Douglass and urged him to accept a position as one of his assistants, publicly to advocate its principles . . . [H]e tried to refuse, but all excuses were swept aside by Mr. Collins, and finally Douglass decided to make a trial for three months. After recovering from his first timidity, he entered the fight with enthusiasm. No one was more surprised than he at his ability to meet the expectations of the people. In the early part of his work he was accompanied by George Foster. They traveled and lectured from the same platform through the eastern counties of Massachusetts. He was frequently introduced to the audiences as a 'chattel,' a 'thing,' a 'piece of property,' and Mr. Collins invariably called their attention to the fact that the speaker was a 'graduate from an institution whose diploma was written upon his back.'"[131]

Garrison's followers had everything to gain by enlisting Douglass under

---

[129] Washington, *F. Douglass*, 71–72.

[130] Fought, *Women*, 70–71.

[131] Washington, *F. Douglass*, 72–73.

their banner, while through them, he found a way for advancement beyond the day work that he had been doing.[132] Douglass's salary was to be $450 a year, ($14,542 in 2022). He was reluctant to accept Collins's offer at first because he was afraid of being arrested and because he doubted his ability as a speaker. In an article copied in *The Liberator* about his speech at the Plymouth County convention in November, he was likened to the rebel gladiator, Spartacus. His stated value to his master at the time was $2,000 ($64,632 in 2022).[133]

---

[132] Parker, "Reminiscences," in Coles, *Cradle*, Chapter XXXIII, 160.
[133] Holland, *F. D. Colored Orator*, 59–60; and U.S. Inflation Calculator for 1841.

CHAPTER 20

Not an Exhibit

According to Washington, Douglass "soon persuaded his friends and associates to think that he was too much of a man to be employed as a mere 'exhibit.' At first his eloquence and success with the public both delighted and alarmed them. There began to arise a fear that his power as an orator would prove too great. It seemed well enough for him to tell the story of his servitude, but when he indulged in logic and flights of fancy and invective, it was feared that he would be considered an impostor. If slavery was such a degrading thing as this man said it was, the question naturally arose, How, then, did he acquire his accomplishments? Besides, Douglass did not give the name of his master, or the state from which he came. All this was true enough, and the truth was somewhat embarrassing, but the people did not stop to consider the omission. Douglass was now a resident of Massachusetts; he was a slave, owned in Maryland. To state the facts about his identity would be to invite slave-catchers to New Bedford to reclaim strayed property. There was nothing for him to do but to keep the dangerous secret securely locked in his own bosom and talk down the doubts and suspicions that were now and then expressed. George Foster, Mr. Garrison, Mr. Collins, and other friends . . . were always admonishing him not to appear too intelligent, too oratorical, or too logical, lest his claim of having been a slave be discredited. 'Give the facts,' they said, 'and we will take care of the philosophy.' 'Let us have the facts only.' 'Tell your story, Frederick; people will not believe you were ever a slave, if you go on in this way.' 'Be yourself.' 'Better have a little plantation dialect than not.' 'It is not best that you should seem so learned.'

Washington continued, "Such were the complaints and warnings that came to him from those who most admired him, during the first few months of his career as an orator. The young man could scarcely curb his impatience, so great was his moral earnestness. The thoughts which he uttered flowed so spontaneously and uncontrollably from his lips, that it seemed to him he could no more limit himself than he could stop the force of gravitation. Speaking of this embarrassment he says: 'It was impossible for me to repeat the same old story month after month and keep up my interest in it. I could not follow the injunction of my friends, for I was now reading and thinking. New views of the subject were being presented to my mind: I could not always curb my moral indignation.'

"In order to remove all doubts as to whether he was a slave, he put the facts, including the name of his master, in the possession of the Anti-Slavery Society. As soon as [Wendell] Phillips [a member of the AASS] and Garrison knew the truth, they advised him to go on as before, for if he gave his name and that of his master, he would be in danger of recapture—even in Massachusetts. When he showed to Wendell Phillips a manuscript detailing the facts of his slave-life, he was advised 'to throw it in the fire'; but so straightforward and earnest and effective was his work, and so rapid his development as an orator, that he soon overcame all doubts, and those who had once urged him to curb his intellectual flights learned to admire his courage, and to put a higher value on his services to the cause of Abolition. Whenever there was serious work to be done, and the best men and women were needed to combat pro-slavery policies and measures, he was eagerly sought. His name now began to be announced with those of the foremost advocates of freedom."[134]

Douglass could have become a minister, in which case, Anna would have taken on the duties of a minister's wife, and her status and respectability would have risen. But Douglass couldn't stand the outright or quiet tolerance for slavery in most churches and chose to keep his faith without joining any denomination. He began to see himself as a black William Lloyd Garrison, working for the betterment of his race and supporting his family.[135]

Twice in September 1841, Douglass was insulted and/or physically thrown off the Eastern Railroad. One time in Lynn, when Collins, his white traveling

---

[134] Washington, *F. Douglass*, 73–75.
[135] Fought, *Women*, 57, and 71.

companion, objected to Douglass's being harassed, Collins, too, was ordered off the train. When Collins objected, the conductor called five men to remove them; Douglass's clothes were ripped and Collins was roughed up. A second time at the train depot in Lynn, when Douglass boarded a train and sat down with white passengers—Collins's abolitionist friend, a former Quaker and Lynn neighbor, James N. Buffum, and an unidentified female abolitionist—the same conductor grabbed Douglass by the collar and ordered him to the colored car. Douglass demanded the reason, and argued with the conductor. Then when five railroad company toughs began to pull Douglass and Collins out of their seat, Douglass held tight to the seat until it was ripped out of the floor. Then he, Collins, and the seat were thrown out the door and off the train, followed by Douglass's luggage.

    Blight wrote that people in Lynn held meetings to protest the way Douglass had been treated on the train. Garrison's followers protested widely and one local newspaper supported Douglass and the other abolitionists. Douglass understood that he had become the public face of a victim of Yankee racism. For those reasons, including that he was no longer a day laborer, Douglass planned to move to Lynn, where the town made an effort to welcome the young celebrity. Blight wrote that the American Anti-Slavery Society helped him either buy or build a house there. Douglass's son, Charles, later wrote that the cottage had been built with his father's own hands, on Union Street, in the heart of town at the intersection of Exchange Street and the railroad, which was a short walk from the depot. Although the Douglasses had moved from New Bedford to Lynn, Anna returned to New Bedford for Fred Jr.'s birth in March 1842, Blight suggested possibly because of support from friends or a midwife.[136]

    Douglass's work changed as he stepped away from prominence in a black community to apprenticeship in mostly white groups, and from day jobs to traveling for speaking engagements. When the Douglass family eventually moved about seventy miles from New Bedford to Lynn, its anti-slavery society and ladies' anti-slavery society were very active, but mostly white. Frederick and Anna found a strong black community, six miles away in Salem (with a

---

[136] Blight, *F. D. Prophet,* 110–11.

population in 1840 of about 15,000), which actively opposed slavery and segregation. The move to Lynn was hard for Anna, who left a safe and welcoming community just as Frederick traveled more often.[137]

Lynn was the largest city in Essex County, a Quaker town with a wide view of shipping lanes. It had a population in 1840 of about 9,000 and was a quick train ride from Boston to the Anti-Slavery offices. Its residents were mostly white and progressive, but Douglass spent little time at home because of traveling. With help from friends, he bought Anna a horse and buggy, and sent her money. She took care of the house and children, and worked as a domestic.[138]

Douglass traveled across New England for the Rhode Island and Massachusetts anti-slavery societies for four years. He also visited New York and Pennsylvania twice and Ohio and Indiana once. He went to annual meetings of the American Anti-Slavery Society in New York City where the middle-class values of abolitionists in the late 1830s and early 1840s weren't the norm, and their gatherings of men and women of both races attracted attackers who disrupted the speakers. White women could count on men to protect them, but black women couldn't and had their bonnets and shawls ripped off. According to Bjornlund, women had been excluded from politics since colonial times in the belief that they were intellectually unfit and that their delicate nature suited them only for home and hearth. The rigors of the American Revolution had driven women to take on non-traditional roles, but their hopes of achieving a better status in society didn't come to pass in the early 1800s. Most women still believed they belonged at home.[139]

By the time of the Nantucket speech, women had sustained the anti-slavery movement for years. They formed the Boston Female Anti-Slavery Society, which was integrated from its beginning in 1838. These women teamed up with their sister society in Philadelphia and linked arms against a rioting mob that burned down the hall where they met. They stood up for Douglass, walked out when he wasn't allowed in public places, and gave him food and shelter as

---

[137] Fought, *Women*, 57–58.

[138] Burchard, *F. Douglass*, 80; McFeely, *F. D.*, 92; Fought, *Women*, 57; and Maryann Weidt, *Voice of Freedom* (Minneapolis: Carolrhoda Books, 2001), 35–37.

[139] Bjornlund, *Women of Colonial America*, 80, 94; and Fought, *Women*, 71.

an equal in their homes. Black and white women who sheltered abolitionists had no sympathy or protection from law enforcers since their political actions were unacceptable. Anti-abolitionists, irate at the threat to conventional rule and private property ownership of white men, saw all women abolitionists as undeserving of the protection given to middle-class white women. Women participating in public gatherings went against the norm of women's involvement in politics being indelicate and unladylike—a convention that Douglass had to overcome, Fought wrote. After speaker Abby Kelley was elected to the executive board of the American Anti-Slavery Society in 1841, a group broke off that didn't accept women in leadership except as auxiliaries. Kelley's behavior was considered outrageous at a time when women's names were publicized only when they married and died. Wherever Douglass went, women served as leaders and expressed strong opinions in women-only and mixed-gender groups.[140]

"In the Rhode Island campaign," Washington wrote," the anti-slavery societies massed their forces and went into the little state to dispute every inch of the ground. Stephen S. Foster, Parker Pillsbury, Abby Kelley, James Monroe, and Frederick Douglass were the advance guard. The contest here was somewhat different from the more or less peaceful work of holding public meetings in Massachusetts to create public opinion. Here was a clean-cut issue in which was involved the right of free Negroes to be full citizens in a Northern state. Under the leadership of Thomas W. Dorr, the pro-slavery forces had to be opposed by strong arguments and not by mere sentiment. There was also a decided feeling against 'intermeddlers,' as Douglass and his associates were called. Meetings were held all over the state, and soon it was plain to be seen that the anti-slavery people were making progress in overcoming the 'Dorrites.' It was a picturesque and dramatic campaign, the chief features of which were the conspicuous parts taken by Frederick Douglass, the fugitive slave, and Abby Kelley. Mr. Douglass says that she 'was perhaps the most successful of any of us. Her youth and simple Quaker beauty, combined with her wonderful earnestness, her large knowledge and great logical powers bore down all opposition to the

---

[140] Fought, *Women*, 71–74.

end, wherever she spoke, though she was before pelted with foul eggs, and no less foul words, from the noisy mobs which attended us.'"[141]

To the best of Douglass's recall, he met activist Elizabeth Cady Stanton in 1841 at a meeting of the Boston Female Anti-Slavery Society where she had confronted him after the gathering. Stanton explained the great injustice of women not having the right to vote for those who made laws that shaped people's lives regardless of gender. At the time Douglass hadn't thought much about the topic, believing in conventional ideas of "women's sphere" and "natural division of duties." Years later, in their book, *The History of Woman Suffrage*, neither Susan B. Anthony nor Stanton remembered his being introduced to women's causes before the convention at Seneca Falls in 1848. The differences in their memories could be because of his experiences in a civil rights movement led mostly by black men and theirs in a women's movement led mostly by white women.[142]

---

[141] Washington, *F. Douglass*, 76–77.
[142] Fought, *Women*, 152.

CHAPTER 21

Attacks Against Hypocrisy

For three years, Douglass endured long hours on trains, on horseback, or in carriages, and stayed in so many people's homes that he knew fifteen families in Rhode Island. Anna passed him clean clothes and food as his train went through town. From late March to early May 1842, he spoke in forty small towns in eastern and central Massachusetts. His speech at Faneuil Hall in Boston in 1842 was so powerful, that years later, Elizabeth Cady Stanton remembered it clearly. Douglass's most popular subject, Blight wrote, was the "Slaveholder's Sermon" in which Douglass mocked Methodist preachers' Biblically based commands, "Servants, obey your masters." His wit, sarcasm, and attacks against the hypocrisy of churches kept audiences spellbound for hours. Directly from that tour he went to New York City and spoke before a crowd of 3,000 attendees at the American Anti-Slavery Society (AASS) annual convention at the Broadway Tabernacle where he most likely met physician James McCune Smith, the most educated black man of his time.[143]

At the AASS convention in New York City in May 1842, Douglass, Phillips, and Kelley introduced a resolution, stating that "The cause of human rights imperatively demands the dissolution of the American Union." Despite 250 of Garrison's supporters having been at the convention, the resolution failed to pass. Garrison had sensed the opposition and didn't attend the convention, but he did send a letter supporting the dissolution of the Union. At a later Boston convention, abolitionism became linked with disunionism.[144]

---

[143] Blight, *F. D. Prophet*, 112, 114, and 116.
[144] Holland, *F. D. Colored Orator*, 70.

The annual meeting of the American Anti-Slavery Society usually met at the same time as the Philadelphia Yearly Meeting that Quaker Lucretia Mott attended. In 1842, Mott attended an Anti-Sabbath Convention in Boston organized by William Lloyd Garrison. Anti-Sabbath reformers claimed that strict observance of the Sabbath deprived working people of time for recreation on their one day of rest. These reformers stated there were no strict rules in the New Testament about it. Mott restricted her activities to light sewing on Sundays, and gave up attending some Sabbath meetings to visit black families and poor women instead. She agreed with Garrison's goals for the convention, went to it and spoke several times. After the trip to Boston, she attended the AASS's annual meeting for the first time in ten years. In her speech, "The Law of Progress," she shared her growing belief that there was only one Christ, but many Messiahs, and compared modern abolitionists to Jesus. The press condemned the speech which was used for many years against her as an example of heresy.[145]

---

[145] Margaret Hope Bacon, *Valiant Friend: The Life of Lucretia Mott* (New York: Walker and Co., 1980) 118–120.

CHAPTER 22

Personal vs. Public Life

In Massachusetts, Frederick and Anna Douglass were adjusting to their new life. According to Fought, each had worked under white owners or employers who ignored their right to a personal life. Neither had rights as workers, and black women who worked in public were scorned. For the first time as an adult, Anna enjoyed privacy in her own home. But, as Frederick became better known, their home life and marriage came under scrutiny. As he needed more quiet to prepare speeches, setting boundaries about who entered their home became a sore point.[146]

In the early 1900s, Rosetta Douglass Sprague described her mother as a staunch worker in the anti-slavery societies of Lynn and Boston. Rosetta would have been young at the time—three to six years old—and believed that anti-slavery society women helped Anna so she could attend weekly meetings where she helped with refreshments and set aside some of her earnings as donations. Fought wrote that there are no records of Anna attending any meetings. Most women activists didn't have several children like Anna, who had three, nor did they work outside the home. White middle-class women were frowned on for being paid to work, and those doing acceptable charitable work may have looked on Anna as a charity case. Their help may have been thinly veiled judgements of Anna's abilities. If the help were sincere, Anna might have accepted it; but if it were patronizing, then it was offensive.[147]

After the American Anti-Slavery Society set a goal in 1843 of holding one hundred anti-slavery meetings that year, Douglass volunteered for the tour. He

---

[146] Fought, *Women*, 56, and 58.
[147] Fought, *Women*, 59, and 329 (note 39).

nearly reached that goal in New England, upstate New York, Ohio, Indiana, and Pennsylvania.[148]

Rhode Island was a hot bed for the slave trade between the West Indies and Africa. Rhode Islanders distilled rum from molasses, sent the rum to Africa to trade for slaves, and then traded them in the West Indies for more molasses. In the years after the American Revolution, despite laws against slave trading, Rhode Island merchants controlled between sixty and ninety percent of the American trade in Africans. Rhode Island's economy thrived from the Triangle Trade between Africa and Cuba, and it took Rhode Island until the mid-1800s to embrace abolition.[149]

Washington wrote, "Yet it was not all smooth sailing for the colored orator. He was frequently dragged from the [train] cars by mobs, though his associates were always loyal to him, many of them refusing to go where he could not. This was especially the case with Wendell Phillips, James Monroe, and William A. White. The result of the battle in Rhode Island [to end slavery] was a complete triumph over those who had sought to abridge the suffrage. The victory was not only important, as a show of strength of the Abolitionists, but it prevented the establishment of a dangerous precedent which might have had its influence upon other states."[150]

Douglass and other black speakers were paid less than white speakers and privately seen by organizers as talented but not trustworthy. Angry mobs harassed black and white speakers with insults, stones, and eggs. While he was away and earning low pay, Anna took in piecework, stitching shoe tops to soles for local factories and living in dread of deadly harm to him.[151]

"At one time when he, with Garrison, Abby Kelley, and [Stephen] Foster, attempted to speak in Hartford, Connecticut, the doors of every hall and church were closed against them," Washington wrote, "but they spoke under the open sky, to so much effect that some of their opponents had the grace to confess to

---

[148] McFeely, *F. Douglass*, 104.

[149] Douglas Harper, slavenorth.com: "Slavery in Rhode Island," 2003; and J. Stanley Lemons, *Rhode Island History: The Slave Trade*, 60, issue 4 (Nov. 2002): 94–104.

[150] Washington, *F. Douglass*, 77.

[151] Fought, *Women*, 58–60.

a sense of shame for such action. At Grafton, Massachusetts, Douglass was advertised to speak alone. There was no house, church, or market-place in which he was permitted to appear. Not to be outdone, he went up and down the streets ringing a dinner-bell that he had borrowed, announcing that 'Frederick Douglass, recently a slave, will lecture on Grafton Common this evening at seven o'clock.' As a result of this notice, he spoke to a great concourse of people, and as usual advanced the cause of Abolition."[152]

---

[152] Washington, *F. Douglass*, 78.

CHAPTER 23

The Abolitionists's Circle

A year after his first major public speech in Nantucket, Douglass returned to abolitionist conventions in New Bedford and Nantucket. Anti-abolition mobs shouted down the speakers in New Bedford, but in Nantucket, mobs shouted and screamed on the first day, and on the second, pelted Garrison, Douglass, and Foster with so many rotten eggs that they shut down the meeting. By this time, Douglass had developed one of his best rebuttals about prayer: that all his praying for freedom as a slave brought him nothing until he *did* something about it and fled. Many churches and town halls were closed to the traveling abolitionists because of Kelley's presence. They met wherever they could in groves, in meadows, and on town greens. After a short stop at home, Douglass left for a two-month crusade through New York State with seven others, including Kelley, dubbed the "moral Joan of Arc of the world."[153]

The lecture circuit brought Douglass in contact with other prominent abolitionists. In May 1842, he met Lucretia Mott at the American Anti-Slavery Society convention in New York City. By then, Mott was well known in abolitionist circles. Mott and her daughter, Anna Hopper, had led a delegation of seventeen women to the first annual Anti-Slavery Convention of American Women, in New York City in May 1837. Mott had organized the three-day convention with Maria W. Chapman, leader of the women's anti-slavery group in Boston.[154]

Douglass most likely met escaped slave and prominent abolitionist Jermain Wesley Loguen of Syracuse, New York, for the first time in the fall of 1842

---

[153] Blight, *F. D. Prophet*, 119–21.
[154] Bryant, *Lucretia* Mott, 98, and 103.

while on a speaking tour across New York State with Kelley.[155] The causes dear to Douglass's heart were abolition, equal rights for blacks, and women's rights.[156]

Over the course of four years, Douglass witnessed the efforts that women gave to the cause, from sewing items for fairs, to serving as officers in mixed-gender meetings, to full-fledged leaders like Kelley and Chapman, often at personal risk.[157]

When Kelley and Douglass first met in 1841, she was one of a few women lecturers. Fought wrote that after she had been elected to the executive board of the American Anti-Slavery Society (AASS), the group split into two and the new organization didn't accept women in leadership, except in auxiliaries. Kelley and Douglass toured for weeks in November and December 1841 in Rhode Island; from August to October 1842 in New York State; and elsewhere in August 1843. Unlike most women anti-slavery advocates, who worked locally and behind the scenes, Kelley lectured publicly, which was a new experience for Douglass.

Kelley was raised a Quaker. In 1836, when she was a teacher, she joined the Lynn Ladies' Anti-Slavery Society in Massachusetts. Fought wrote that as its corresponding secretary, she joined petitioning campaigns at a time when it was disgraceful for women's names to appear in print. She had been inspired by the Grimké sisters and had taken to public speaking after a mob destroyed the Friends' Pennsylvania Hall in Philadelphia in 1838. During her first years of lecturing, she was labeled disreputable, but, by 1842, she was in high demand as a speaker by supporters and women's groups. Douglass recognized that coordinating secretaries were key organizers of petition drives, which he said delighted "the hearts of slaves." He saw that these women, who usually were in integrated groups, also solicited donors, speakers, and newspaper subscribers. Fought continued, the contrast between their styles—Kelley's "simple Quaker beauty . . . and wonderful earnestness" and Douglass's commanding presence and caustic wit—was sensational. In 1842, Quaker sisters Lydia and Abigail

---

[155] Douglass, *F. D. Papers*. Series three, Correspondence, vol.1, 474 (note 1).

[156] Philip Foner, *Life and Writings of Frederick Douglass* (New York: International Publishers, 1950), 15.

[157] Fought, *Women*, 74–78.

Mott warned Kelley, "Caution as you are traveling about with Fred Douglas[s]," because of the violent reactions people had to the sight of them in public. During their first months on tour, Kelley and Douglass were insulted verbally and physically. Through the efforts of dedicated women, the western and central New York anti-slavery societies formed between 1842 and 1843 because of Kelley's efforts in bringing Douglass across New York State twice. Paulina Wright in Utica, Oneida County, and Amy Post in Rochester, Monroe County, worked diligently to rally supporters.[158]

Across upstate New York, the frontier era after the American Revolution had fostered brotherliness and inter-denominational cooperation. This mutual aid faded by the mid-1830s as groups no longer depended on each other. By the mid-1840s these once-united movements shifted into a political focus against slavery. While Garrison's followers steered away from politics, white evangelicals turned to political action. Uneasy distaste for allying anti-slavery as a cause with religious enthusiasms slowed the movement for a time, but the crusade became the major issue of the century, with no other area of the country being so attuned to anti-slavery activities as upstate New York.[159]

Racial prejudice wasn't as vicious in western New York as other parts of the country, according to black abolitionist and clergyman Samuel R. Ward. But he saw it as a testing ground because blacks could do better there than where they were scorned or ignored. Also, upstate women who worked against slavery challenged gender-based limits before the Civil War.[160]

In March 1842, Amy Post signed and circulated a petition from men and women living in Rochester and surrounding areas that was a shift in women's public advocacy for abolition. Most anti-slavery supporters, who tended to be white women, didn't sign it because, by then, preachers, who tended to be white men, had forbidden women from participating in public political actions. But white evangelical men joined the Liberty Party. Of the signers, sixty-three

---

[158] Fought, *Women*, 74–78.

[159] Whitney R. Cross, The *Burned-Over District: The Social and Intellectual History of Enthusiastic Religion in Western New York, 1800–1850* (New York: Harper Torchbooks, 1950), 225–226.

[160] Milton Sernett, *North Star Country* (Syracuse: Syracuse University Press, 2002), xx.

were women, more than half of them Quakers, and many were signing such a petition for the first time.[161]

By the time Kelley came again to Rochester in August 1842, Isaac and Amy Post and other radical Quakers were key players in the local movement, Hewitt wrote. Kelley, Douglass, and Erasmus Hudson—a white physician who lectured on temperance and abolition—were insulted in public while traveling together. When local abolitionists held their talk in Third Presbyterian Church, the minister objected to a woman as well as a black man, speaking from the pulpit and expelled them. Kelley and Douglass reconvened at African Bethel Church where the Posts were among the attendees. The Posts were eager to see Kelley and to meet Douglass, whom they had agreed to host for the first time. His short visit in their home marked the beginning of a friendship that had a lasting impact on the anti-slavery movement.[162] Douglass spoke for the first time in Rochester, New York, on August 30, 1842.[163]

Kelley and Douglass addressed meetings in nineteen towns across New York State, Blight wrote. They traveled by farm wagon, stagecoach, and carriage, on the Erie Canal, and sometimes by train. In Vienna, Oneida County, they were assaulted with brickbats and stones and, when the meeting was disrupted by a small pig thrown into the hall, they retreated to the railroad depot. In Port Byron, Cayuga County, the crowd of four hundred at the National Hotel was disruptive, "hissing and murmuring." Kelley and Douglass were thrown out of the Baptist meetinghouse in Ithaca, Tompkins County, and moved to the courthouse square, where, eventually, someone climbed the tower and rang the courthouse bell to disrupt them. In September, the only place they could find that would allow them to speak in Trumansburg, Tompkins County, was a tavern. Despite many setbacks, abolitionist teams used newspapers and pamphlets to reach small villages away from the Erie Canal or New York Central Railway lines.[164]

---

[161] Hewitt, *Radical Friend*, 88–89.

[162] Hewitt, *Radical Friend*, 91.

[163] Holland, *F. D. Colored Orator*, 71.

[164] Blight, *F. D. Prophet*, 122–23.

Kelley and Douglass's New York tour ended in late October in Cooperstown, Otsego County. Douglass then went home to Lynn, Massachusetts, for a much-needed rest. After three days though, he rushed to Boston to speak before a crowd of 4,000 about the arrest of a light-skinned black fugitive named George Latimer. After Latimer was freed, abolitionist speakers Garrison, Phillips, Douglass, and Charles Lenox Remond (a Massachusetts abolitionist, friend of Garrison, and the person for whom Douglass's son Charles Remond was named), spoke at rallies across New England. One was so noisy, listeners could hardly hear the speakers. Even so, Douglass and Remond traveled for many days until Douglass became sick and his voice gave out. After one "Latimer meeting," Douglass spoke for an hour, then sat down with a pain in his chest and shortness of breath. While recovering at home, he wrote letters to Garrison for publication in *The Liberator*.[165]

---

[165] Blight, *F. D. Prophet*, 124–25.

CHAPTER 24

An Ambitious Undertaking

"In the year 1843, the movement had so far progressed that a great undertaking was announced," Washington wrote. "It was proposed to hold one hundred conventions under the auspices of the Massachusetts Anti-Slavery Society in such states as New Hampshire, Vermont, New York, Ohio, Indiana, and Pennsylvania. Mr. Douglass was selected as one of the agents to assist in the work. This was regarded as an ambitious scheme on the part of Mr. Garrison, and attracted a great deal of public attention. Among the speakers associated with Mr. Douglass in this tour were George Bradburn, John A. Collins, James Monroe, Sidney Howard Gay, and Charles Lenox Remond, the last-named a colored man of unusual eloquence. Mr. Douglass felt very proud, as well he might, of being given so prominent a part in this important enterprise, and of being associated with men of such distinction. The wisdom of holding these conventions was soon made manifest, when it was discovered how ill-informed were the masses of the people as to the nature of the issue the Abolitionists were seeking to force upon the attention of the country.

"The crusade received rather a chilly reception in the Green Mountain State. Along the Erie Canal, from Albany to Buffalo, it was more than difficult to excite any interest or to make converts. In Syracuse, the home of Rev. Samuel J. May, and where such men as Gerrit Smith, Beriah Green, and William Goodell lived, Douglass and his friends could not obtain a hall, church, or market-place to hold a meeting. Everybody was discouraged and favored 'shaking the dust from off their feet,' and going to other parts. But Frederick Douglass did not believe in surrender. He was determined to speak his word for the gospel of Abolition here, even if he must do so under the open sky, as in Connecticut and Massachusetts. In the morning he began in a grove with five people present. So powerful was his appeal that in the afternoon he had an audience of five hundred and in the evening he was tendered the use of an old building that had done service as a Congregational church. In this house the convention was organized and carried on for three days. The seeds of Abolition were so well sown in Syracuse, that thereafter it was always hospitable ground for anti-slavery advocates. Mr. Douglass had a more friendly reception in Rochester, which was to be his future home. Here he found a goodly number of Abolitionists and his words made a lasting impression.[166]

In June 1843, according to Blight, Douglass wrote that a meeting in New Hampshire had been "disgraceful, alarming, divided, united, glorious, and most effective." Afterward, he went to Lynn to rest before beginning the ambitious "one hundred conventions" tour, which was to take place from July to December. Nearly everywhere the abolitionist speakers went, Liberty Party advocates did everything they could to disrupt their anti-slavery campaign. In Vermont, vicious notices against the speakers were plastered all over Middlebury. Their meeting in Utica, New York, had a low turnout. At first, Douglass traveled alone in Syracuse. But Collins, Kelley, and Remond joined him there for three days, which were marred by Collins diverting the topic from abolition of slavery to abolishing private property. Douglass and Remond countered with heated arguments. Collins and Douglass wrote to the American Anti-Slavery Society board to defend their positions. In the middle of it all, Douglass wrote AASS executive committee member Maria W. Chapman, asking her to send Anna $25 or $30 ($1,001 or $1,201 in 2022), because he had nothing to send her. "He woke every day worrying about how to feed his family as well as how to best use his voice to free his fellow slaves. He struggled mightily to do both," Blight wrote.[167]

Douglass wrote, "In the growing city of Rochester we had in every way a better reception. Abolitionists of all shades of opinion were broad enough to give the Garrisonians (for such we were) a hearing. Samuel D. Porter and the Avery family, though they belonged to the Gerrit Smith, Myron Holley, and

---

[166] Washington, *F. Douglass*, 78–81.
[167] Blight, *F. D. Prophet*, 128–29; and U.S. Inflation Calculator for 1843.

William Goodell school, were not so narrow as to refuse us the use of their church for the convention. They heard our moral suasion arguments, and in a manly way met us in debate. We were opposed to carrying the anti-slavery cause to the ballot-box, and they believed in carrying it there. They looked at slavery as a creature of *law;* we regarded it as a creature of public opinion. It is surprising how small the difference appears as I look back to it, over the space of forty years; yet at the time of it this difference was immense.

"During our stay at Rochester we were hospitably entertained by Isaac and Amy Post, two people of all-abounding benevolence, the truest and best of Long Island and Elias Hicks Quakers. They were not more amiable than brave, for they never seemed to ask, What will the world say? but walked straight forward in what seemed to them the line of duty, please or offend whomsoever it might. Many a poor fugitive slave found shelter under their roof when such shelter was hard to find elsewhere, and I mention them here in the warmth and fullness of earnest gratitude."[168]

Douglass was so happy to return to Rochester, Blight wrote, that before he began a speech there August 5, he delighted the gathering by singing an abolition song. After Syracuse and Rochester, Douglass and Remond planned to travel to Buffalo to reach new audiences.[169]

According to Washington, "The next meeting of importance was in Buffalo. The outlook for a convention in this western New York city was so discouraging that Mr. Douglass'[s] associates turned on their heels and left him to 'do Buffalo alone.' The place appointed was a dilapidated old room that had once been used as a post office. No one was there at first except a few hack drivers who sauntered in from curiosity. But Mr. Douglass went at them with great earnestness, as if they could settle all the problems that were overburdening his heart. Out of this small and unsympathetic beginning, grew a great convention. Every day for nearly a week, in the old building, he spoke to constantly increasing crowds of people, who were worth talking to, until finally a large Baptist church was thrown open to him. Here the size and character of the audience

---

[168] Douglass, *Autobiographies*, 673–74.
[169] Blight, *F. D. Prophet*, 130.

were flattering. So great was the eagerness to hear him that on Sunday evening he addressed an outdoor meeting of five thousand people in the park."[170]

Sally Holley, a daughter of the late abolitionist Myron Holley, was a surprising part of the audience in the post office in Buffalo, Holland wrote. Douglass described her as "a young lady, who brought no escort but a little girl, and who was so beautiful as to look, in that rough crowd, like an angel of light." Douglass didn't expect to see her again, but she came every day, and he learned who she was and that her father, a founder of the Liberty Party, "had been reduced to earning his living" by delivering milk. Sally later wrote that the first time she ever heard Douglass speak, his "soul poured out with rare pathos and power."[171]

Douglass and Remond were in Buffalo, Blight wrote, around the time of the thirteenth annual National Colored Convention. Presbyterian Rev. Henry Highland Garnet, a former slave from Maryland, delivered a riveting address advocating that slaves resist their bondage. Douglass spoke out strongly that insurrection was disastrous. *The Liberator* supported Douglass's public disagreement over the use of violence, as well as his opposition to a resolution declaring it the delegates' duty to vote for the Liberty Party. These events marked the beginning of a long-lasting feud between Douglass and Rev. Garnet. Out of seventy-three delegates, Douglass and Remond were the only ones from Massachusetts, out of the ten states present.[172]

Washington wrote, "From this city [Buffalo] Douglass continued on his way into Ohio and Indiana. The Ohio meeting, held in Clinton County, was a notable event. This was the farthest west Mr. Douglass had been as yet and he now went into the state of Indiana. This was dangerous ground, as he soon learned when he attempted to deliver his message. Here he found a mob spirit harder to resist than any he had encountered in the East. In attempting to speak at Richmond, Ind[iana], where Henry Clay had been heard shortly before, he received a shower of 'evil-smelling eggs.' From this place he went to Pendleton, where he could find no hall or church in which to speak; but, not to be outdone,

---

[170] Washington, *F. Douglass*, 80.
[171] Holland, *F. D. Colored Orator*, 93.
[172] Blight, *F. D. Prophet*, 131.

he attempted what he had successfully accomplished at Syracuse, and at other places. He had a platform erected in the woods. A large assembly of people came out to hear the colored orator, but the Hoosiers, in this part of the state, were determined not to be persuaded.

"It was, as one of them rudely expressed it, a case of "no nigger speaker for us." As soon as the meeting began, a mob of fifty or sixty rough-looking men ordered Douglass to stop. An attempt to disregard this threatening command, maddened the rioters. They tore down the platform and violently assaulted the orator and his associate, Mr. White. Seeing the danger, Douglass began, to fight his way through the crowd with a club. The sight of a weapon in the hands of a Negro angered the mob still more, and they set upon him with such fury that he was felled to the ground, being beaten so fiercely that he was left for dead. Having dispersed the meeting, the men mounted their horses and rode away. Mr. Douglass's right hand was broken, and he was in a state of unconsciousness for some time. He was unable to speak for several days, being tenderly cared for by a Mrs. Neal Hardy, a member of the Society of Friends, until his wounds were healed, but he never recovered the full use of his right hand.

"Notwithstanding this rough treatment, Mr. Douglass would not allow himself to be frightened out of the state. He continued his work for a long time, and compelled a respectful and peaceful hearing. He was no coward and was not afraid of mobs. He did not stop until, according to the plans determined upon by the Anti-Slavery Society of Massachusetts, the one hundred conventions had been held. The work was accomplished, in spite of indifference, contemptuous criticism, and sometimes violent and bloody opposition.

"Although it seemed at the time that not much had been achieved, the seed sown was to bear fruit when a few years later the South and North were arrayed against each other in the great struggle for the preservation of the Union."[173]

"During this tour," Coles wrote, "Mr. Douglass became better acquainted with the technical questions and causes concerning the continuation of one of the richest industries in the United States—the system of slavery. The value of slave property rose to close to two billion dollars. Cotton was "king" and

---

[173] Washington, F, Douglass, 81–82.

represented the basic economic interest of the United States, and the influence of slavery was felt in the social, political and business life. In the North and the South, the business interests' and aims were identical, for both were anxious to preserve slavery because of the huge profits from these human chattels." (Two billion dollars equaled $80,543,243, 243 in 2022).[174]

McFeely wrote about a letter that Douglass later wrote to William White, the anti-slavery agent who had travelled with Douglass and speaker George Bradburn to Pendleton, Indiana, in 1843. While staying as guests at the home of a local physician, they heard a hard-drinking mob planned to disrupt their talks. In the letter, Douglass recalled: "I shall never forget how like two very brothers we were ready to dare, do and even die for each other. Tragic, awfully so, yet I laugh when I think how comic I must have looked when running before the mob, darkening the air with mud from my feet. How I looked running, you can best describe but how you looked bleeding I shall always remember."

White had fallen on the ground, bleeding from a blow that knocked out his teeth. The following week in Jonesboro, Indiana, McFeely wrote, Remond joined Bradburn and Douglass for the annual meeting of the Indiana Anti-Slavery Society. Douglass and Bradburn had a bitter quarrel on stage in which Remond sided with Douglass. Douglass and Remond went on without Bradburn to Clinton County, Ohio, where Douglass got into another fierce public argument. Several in the anti-slavery society considered such behavior disgraceful, while others respected Douglass's right to his own voice under trying conditions. In December, Douglass attended the closing meeting of the Hundred Conventions in Philadelphia, that was also the tenth anniversary of the local American Anti-Slavery Society.[175]

In January 1844, Douglass wrote a letter from Lynn, Massachusetts, to the vice-president of the Bristol County Anti-Slavery Society. Douglass clarified that he had given money to John Collins who had promised aid for the legal expenses of two black men who had been thrown from their seats on the local railroad. During the scuffle, one had drawn a knife and the two were arrested. At

---

[174] Coles, *Cradle*, Chapter XXVIII, 125; and U. S. Inflation Calculator for 1843.
[175] McFeely, *F. Douglass*, 108–113.

the end of January, Douglass attended the Massachusetts Anti-Slavery Society's (MASS) annual meeting in Boston.

In February, Douglass wrote from Lynn to Wendell Phillips about the terms of his continued employment for attending conventions. Well-funded abolitionist groups paid lecturers several ways, including room and board when they traveled, and salaries ranging from $300 to 600 a year (c. $12,000 to $24,000 in 2022). Poorer societies paid speakers from the proceeds of the tour. In 1844, the MASS paid Douglass $142, ($5,600 in 2022) for attending conventions. He was the most highly paid employee that year, yet most traveling lecturers were barely able to support their families.

Toward the end of February, Douglass and Garrison went to Lowell, Massachusetts, for a meeting of the One Hundred Conventions tour. In March, Douglass and others went to Groton, Massachusetts, which had a meeting hall where anti-slavery speakers had been welcomed for several years. Douglass noticed the audience in Groton was much smaller than when he had spoken there two years earlier. He attributed the change to religious fervor about the return of Jesus Christ to earth sometime in 1843 or 1844. He kept Garrison up to date about the accomplishment and setbacks of his latest travels.[176]

While on tour in Pennsylvania, Douglass met Ruth Cox, a slave who had fled from Talbot County, Maryland, to West Chester, Chester County. Quakers in West Chester protected her and gave her work. Cox was the daughter of a free black father and a slave mother, who worked in the Easton home of a U.S. senator. They lived near the jail in Easton, where teenage Frederick had been jailed after his attempted escape from William Freeland's farm. Blight wrote that Douglass may have mistaken her for his own sister, Eliza, whom he had not seen for eight years.

In the fall of 1844, Douglass brought Cox to Lynn, calling her Harriet like his youngest sister, and invited her to live in their small house. Cox took the name Harriet Bailey and the children called her Auntie Harriet. Frederick and Anna considered her a sister. She knew how to read and used skills she had learned in her former owners' townhouse to help Anna. As a southern woman

---

[176] Douglass, *F. D. Papers*. Series three, Correspondence, vol 1, 17–18.

from the same area as Anna, Harriet had a way of doing things and received news from the Eastern Shore that Anna appreciated.[177] Frederick and Anna's son who was born Oct. 21, 1844 was named Charles Remond after Douglass's "closest companion in the crusade": black abolitionist and orator, Charles Lenox Remond.[178]

---

[177] Douglass, *F. D. Papers*. Series three, Correspondence, vol. 1, 125–26; Fought, *Women*, 65–66; and Blight, *F. D. Prophet*, 163–64.
[178] McFeely, *F. Douglass*, 103.

CHAPTER 25

Happiness of Home

"By my own table, in the enjoyment of freedom, and the happiness of home," on Union Street in Lynn, Douglass put the story of his life on paper from December 1844 to May 1845.[179] As a precaution, he never shared his full name and details of his earlier life with his audiences. But when people commented after his speeches that there was no way he had been a slave, he announced after a talk in New Bedford that he would prove that he had. Regarding Douglass's lack of safety, Phillips said in a lecture in March 1845, "God dash the Commonwealth of Massachusetts into a thousand pieces, till there shall not remain a fragment on which an honest man can stand and not dare tell his name." In his *Narrative of the Life of Frederick Douglass, an American Slave*, Douglass described Phillips's recollection of having told Douglass to throw his manuscript into the fire.[180] Douglass retold this story in May 1845 at the annual meeting of the AASS in New York City.[181]

Rochester neighbor Jane Marsh Parker later wrote about Douglass. As a "Methodist exhorter he had learned to speak so fluently and well that it was no wonder that many who heard him in the anti-slavery meetings had doubts if he had ever been a slave, and said so openly."[182]

Washington wrote, "When Frederick Douglass had concluded his remarkable tour from Vermont to Indiana he was one of the most popular and widely

---

[179] Blight, *F. Douglass,* 137. Holland, *F. D. Colored Orator,* 102–103.
[180] Holland, *F. D. Colored Orator,* 102–103.
[181] Douglass, *Autobiographies,* chronology, 1056.
[182] Parker, "Reminiscences," in Coles, *Cradle,* Chapter XXXIII, 160.

talked of men on the American platform. The public everywhere was eager to learn everything possible about the 'runaway slave' who was winning his place among the foremost of American orators. Interest in him was further enhanced by the publication of his 'Narrative,' in 1845. Its issue was made necessary by the demand for something definite concerning the antecedents of this 'alleged slave.' His accomplishments as a speaker and as a reasoner seemed inconsistent with the representation made by him, that he had had no schooling, and that he had been a slave until he was twenty-one years of age. There was a desire for the exact facts. Yet to give them was dangerous. His growing popularity was likewise a peril. The possibility of his capture and return to slavery increased with his influence as an orator and agitator. After this publication, personal friends and the leaders of the anti-slavery cause became more and more apprehensive. It would have been regarded as little less than a calamity to have had Frederick Douglass, the incomparable orator, the man in whom almost for the first time, the silent, toiling slaves had found a voice, dragged back into bondage. Under the circumstances it was deemed expedient for him to go to England."[183]

The Liberator announced the publication of *Narrative* in its lead editorial in early May while the book was being printed, stressing the author wrote it entirely. At its annual meeting in May, the New England Anti-Slavery Society promoted the upcoming book, which was widely covered by the press. Because newspapers and magazines reviewed and praised *Narrative* in the United States, the United Kingdom, and Europe, it was considered the most widely reviewed black autobiography before the Civil War.[184]

The anti-slavery office in Boston published 5,000 of *Narrative* in June 1845 and sold them for $.50 a copy ($19 in 2022). By the fall, 4,500 sold in the United States. *Narrative* included a preface by William Lloyd Garrison in which he described the first time he had ever heard Douglass speak at the anti-slavery convention in Nantucket in 1841. The book also contained a letter from Wendell Phillips, asking Douglass if he remembered the fable, "The Man and the Lion," in which the lion complained that he would not be so misrepresented

---

[183] Washington, *F. Douglass*, 99–100.

[184] Douglass, *F. D. Papers*. Series two, *Narrative*, vol. 1, xxxiii.

"when the lions wrote history." Philips wrote, "I am glad the time has come when 'lions write history.' We have been left long enough to gather the character of slavery from the involuntary evidence of the masters."[185] Both Garrison and Philips remembered Douglass's image of white sailing ships on Chesapeake Bay as a symbol of his longing for freedom and recognized they had read a remarkable work.[186]

Douglass was well into his speaking tour when he heard that slaveholders in Talbot County, Maryland, were furious. A man, who had known Frederick Bailey during the time he had worked under Edward Covey, considered Douglass nothing but a lowly slave and defended the character of Colonel Lloyd, Thomas Auld, and others.[187]

A Rochester newspaper mentioned on July 23, 1845, that "Frederick Douglass, The eloquent fugitive from Southern slavery, will lecture at Tallman Hall, in this city, on Wednesday and Thursday next, at 3 o'clock p.m." Despite the risk to his safety from having named his owners, Douglass went on a lecture tour by himself across New England and New York State from July until his departure in August for his speaking tour in Great Britain.[188]

---

[185] Douglass, *Autobiographies,* preface, 3, 11–13, and chronology 1056; and U.S. Inflation Calculator for 1845.

[186] Douglass, *Autobiographies,* 8, and 11.

[187] Preston, *Young F. D.*, 171.

[188] Whitacre, *A Civil Life*, 20–21.

CHAPTER 26

Travel Abroad

There was a "great gathering" on August 15 at Lyceum Hall in Lynn, Massachusetts, for a farewell party for Douglass, James N. Buffum, and the Hutchinson Family Singers. Douglass brought with him paperback copies of his book to sell at $.25 each or $2.75 a dozen ($9 or $99 in 2022).[189] Boston Anti-Slavery Society leaders had chosen Buffum as Douglass's traveling companion to Ireland, England, and Scotland. Although Buffum had booked a double room in first class on a steam packet called the *Cambria*, the shipping agent wouldn't let a black man travel with whites. Douglass and Buffum downgraded to a small room in steerage and sailed from Boston on August 16, 1845. The mild-mannered white abolitionist smoothed bumps along the way and handled their money.[190]

From steerage, Douglass could visit the rest of the ship except for the first-class stateroom. He took long walks alone on the upper decks, later writing, "You cannot write the bloody laws of slavery on those restless billows. The ocean, if not the land, is free." If the seas were too rough, Douglass and Buffum went to the second-class saloon with the Hutchinson Family Singers, where they could play billiards or shuffleboard on the eleven-day crossing.[191]

The white musical quartet known as the Hutchinson Family Singers included Judson, John Wallace, Asa, and Abigail Jemina Hutchinson, four of Jesse and Polly Hutchinson's thirteen children. Douglass had met them when

---

[189] Blight, *F. D. Prophet*, 139, and U.S. Inflation Calculator for 1845.

[190] Douglass, *F. D. Papers*. Series three, Correspondence, vol. 1, 77 (note 11); and McFeely, *F. Douglass*, 120.

[191] Burchard, *F. Douglass*, 90; and Douglass, *Autobiographies*, 371.

they performed around Lynn, Massachusetts, and he encouraged them to join the movement. The Hutchinsons Singers' parents were ordinary farmers from Milford, New Hampshire. The quartet became well-respected performers who sang about idealism, reforms, equal rights, self-improvement, activism and love of country.[192]

The sky was clear and the sea was calm on the last day of the crossing of the *Cambria*, when Captain Judkins invited Douglass to talk to interested travelers. Among the crowd that gathered were American slaveholders who had been drinking heavily. Douglass spoke strongly about ships that carried human cargo, while hecklers interrupted him repeatedly and then rushed at him with clenched fists. According to English newspapers, after one threatened to throw Douglass overboard, Captain Judkins knocked the assailant down. Word of Douglass's safe arrival spread quickly. After the *Cambria* docked in Liverpool, Douglass, Buffum, and the Hutchinson singers stayed in a hotel for two days without problem. Although Douglass wrote in his memoirs as if he were traveling alone, Douglass and Buffam sailed on the *Cambria* across the Irish Sea to Dublin to meet Richard D. Webb, a publisher and staunch anti-slavery activist.[193] Douglass wrote of visiting "the land of my paternal ancestors."[194]

---

[192] http://www.amaranthpublishing.com/hutchinson.html

[193] Burchard, *F. Douglass*, 90–91; and McFeely, *F. D.*, 120.

[194] Preston, *Young F. D.*, A Douglass Chronology, 1945, 201.

Afterword

I enjoyed the authentic style of Frederic May Holland's, *Frederick Douglass: The Colored Orator*. But it surprised me how he ended the revised 1895 biography saying, "It must have been from his mother's race that he inherited his love of music and mimicry, his open-handed generosity, his warmth of religious feeling, his habitual courtesy, and that loyal gratitude in which he readily overlooked defects in other champions of the oppressed. Few men have been so great and at the same time so lovable, or have left behind them so few enemies and so many friends." So few enemies? There was a time when thousands would have rejoiced at his lynching! Whatever Holland's assessment of "few enemies and so many friends," there is no doubt that Frederick Douglass's influence was deep and wide. But the story could be wider.

My interest in the times in which the Douglass family lived grew from reading a biography in the 1960s of Martin de Porres of Lima, Peru (1579–1639). De Porres was the son of a Black/native mother and a Spanish conquistador. De Porres became the patron saint of interracial justice because of his lineage and his great goodness. Although I'd lost sight of this remarkable man, once I read that Douglass had had native ancestors, I was curious to know more and sought information from better- and lesser-known sources to get a clearer picture of what the family's life was like.

I am grateful to Celeste-Marie Bernier, PhD, co-author of *If I Survive*, who coined the word "invisibilization" to describe the pervasive process of omitting, denying, and minimizing the roles of Black women and men in accounts of national history.[195] Also, according to Dr. Joy DeGruy, constant attempts over the centuries to break the will of slaves in the belief that whites were superior to blacks "absolutely, categorically destroyed existing relationships and undermined a people's ability to form healthy new ones." Just as studies of survivors

---

[195] Celeste-Marie Bernier and Andrew Taylor, *If I Survive: Frederick Douglass and Family in the Walter O. Evans Collection*, (Edinburgh: Edinburgh University Press, 2018) xxxi.

of the Holocaust showed that their trauma was passed on to succeeding generations, the legacy of American slavery can alter genetic codes and is called Post Traumatic Slavery Syndrome.[196]

When Bernier was in Rochester to promote her book in September 2018, she encouraged me to visit an exhibit of rare items about the Douglass family in the National Library of Scotland in Edinburgh. It was a long way to go, but I went. On the last day of the trip, I understood what I had needed to learn—why the Douglass family matters to American history and to today's history.

As a family, they faced the same problems most people do—where to live; what to eat and wear; how to pay bills; how to get along with each other and with those in one's circle; and how to end the curse of slavery. Their circle included many whose roles have been invisibilized. It also became important to see how the wider circle of activists and agitators often did not see eye-to-eye.

The trauma of living in the twisted heart of slavery added weight to the Douglass family's story. This study is of a greater picture than most of us ever get to see. To use a nineteenth-century expression, it's time to "acknowledge the corn," tell the truth about the old days and heal old wounds.

When my book, *Frederick and Anna Douglass in Rochester, New York* was published in 2013, scholars considered it groundbreaking for including Douglass's wife and children. In 2018, the 200th anniversary of his birth, interest in this famous speaker soared with books that also included female abolitionists and reformers from that time. Now, as our nation and world come to grips with buzz words like diversity, equity, and inclusion, I still prefer plain English: all rights for all.

Rose O'Keefe
Rochester, New York

---

[196] DeGruy, *Post Traumatic Slave Syndrome*, 100.

About the Author

Rose O'Keefe is the author of five history books, including two about Frederick and Anna Douglass and their children in Rochester, New York. Rose is a member of Toastmasters International and several writers and neighborhood groups. She and her husband have two grown children, two grandchildren, and two cats.

Her last book was the second edition of *Special Delivery: From One Stop to Another on the Underground Railroad*, set in 1852. Her other books are *Frederick and Anna Douglass in Rochester, New York: Their Home Was Open to All*; *Historic Genesee Country*; *Southeast Rochester*; and *Rochester's South Wedge*.

Index

abolition 26, 36, 44, 49–55, 57–61, 65, 69, 72–79
abolitionism xiv, 62
abolitionist(s) xi, xiii, xiv–xv, 36, 63
  anti- 59, 60
  Black 49–50, 69, 79
  female/women 58, 60–61, 67–68
    see also Kelley, Abby; Mott, Lucretia C. life of an 44–45
  paper xvii, 49 see also Liberator, The
  Quaker xv, 60, 68
  Rhode Island campaign xv, 60–61, 65
  "undertaking" 72–79
  white 51, 52, 53, 83
  see also Garrison, William Lloyd; Phillips, Wendell; Smith, James McCune
Africa x, xix–xxi, 5, 51, 65
African Methodist Episcopal Zion xi, xiv, 46, 50, 51, 52
African(s) x, xix–xxi, 1, 65
  see also Black(s)
Alabama 16, 33
Aliceanna Street 19, 39
AME churches xi, xiv, 36, 42, 46, 50, 51, 52

American Anti-Slavery Society (AAAS) xiii, xvi, 36, 58, 59, 60, 62–63, 64–65, 67, 68, 73, 77, 80
American Nations: A History of the Eleven Rival Regional Cultures of North America xx
American Revolution 2, 8, 59, 65, 69
American Union xv, 62
Annapolis 4, 10, 12, 18
Anthony, Aaron (Captain) 15, 17
  birth x
  children 20 see also Auld, Lucretia
  death xii, 10, 19–20
  early life and marriage 10
  father of Bailey, Frederick 11
  house of 13–14
  slaves of x, xi, xii, 5, 7, 10–12, 16, 20–21
Anthony, Susan B. xi, 61
Anti-Sabbath Convention xv, 63
Anti-Slavery Convention xiv, xvi, 54, 67, 81
anti-slavery movement xi, xiii–xvi, 59, 69–79
  advocates 54–55, 57, 68, 73

campaigns xv, 49, 60–61, 65, 68, 73
cause xiv, 49, 74, 81
disruptions 59, 70, 73, 77 *see also* mob
lawyer 51–52
lectures/speeches xiv–xvi, 22, 50–51, 53–55, 62, 65–66, 70, 72–79
meetings xv–xvi, 50, 54, 60, 64–65, 67, 70, 80
in New Bedford 49–55
office 59, 81
"one hundred conventions" tour 72–79
societies 46 *see also* Anti-Slavery Society
Anti-Slavery Society
   American xiii, xvi, 36, 58, 59, 60, 62–63, 64–65, 67, 68, 73, 77, 80
   Boston Female xiii, xv, 59, 61, 64, 67, 83
   Bristol County 46, 52, 77
   Indiana 77
   Massachusetts xv, 52, 53, 54, 59, 72, 76, 78
   New England xiii, 81
   New York City 80
Assing, Ottilie 41
attacks/assaults xiii, 34, 57–58, 61, 65, 67, 70, 75, 76
Auld, Hugh xii, xiii, 19, 20, 22, 23, 25–27, 33, 34, 42, 43

Auld, Lucretia xii, 13, 14, 17–20, 22
Auld, Rowena 28
Auld, Sophia xii, xiii, 18, 19–20, 22–23, 27, 39
Auld, Thomas xii, xiii, 13, 17, 20, 27–31, 33, 42, 52, 82
Auld, Tommy 18, 19, 20, 23, 40

Bailey, Betsey x, 3, 4, 5, 6–7, 11, 13, 16, 20, 21, 41
Bailey, Eliza 4, 14, 20, 21, 28, 78
Bailey, Frederick Augustus Washington (Douglass) ix–xv, 38, 82
   ancestors ix–x, 2, 3, 4–7, 10–11
   anti-slavery speeches by xiv–xvi, 50–51, 53–55, 62, 65–66, 70, 72–79
   apprenticeship xiii, 34–35, 58
   autobiographies xvi, 6–7, 11, 12, 15, 45
   at Baltimore with the Aulds xii, 18, 19–29
   a bi-racial child 11–12
   birth ix, xi, 5, 10
   a caulker xiii, xiv, 34, 41, 43, 44, 48
   challenges of escape faced by 35, 44
   childhood 6–7, 13–14
   children of xiv, xv, xvi, 5, 52, 58, 79 *see also* Douglass, Charles
   churches attended by xiii, xiv, 25, 36, 48, 50

a colored orator 56–57, 65–66, 72, 76, 81
embarrassment as a speaker 53, 54, 56, 57
escape attempts by xii, xiii, xiv, 32, 44, 78
an exhorter 50, 80
family life in Massachusetts 47, 52, 64
father of *see* Anthony, Aaron (Captain)
a field hand xiii, 30–33
fighting back Covey xiii, 30
financial struggles as a speaker 59, 73
grandfather *see* Bailey, Isaac
grandmother *see* Bailey, Betsey
joining the anti-slavery community 49–55
on Kelley, Abby 60–61
learning to read xii, 22–24
life at Lloyd's plantation 13–14, 15
marriage to Murray, Anna xi, xiv, 40–41, 45
masters of *see* Anthony, Aaron (Captain); Auld, Thomas; Covey, Edward; Freeland, William
meeting Murray, Anna xiv, 37, 40, 42
member of Improvement Society 36–37
mother *see* Bailey, Harriet

move to New Bedford xiv, 46–48
name change xiv, 45, 47
"one hundred conventions" tour 72–79
physical assault of xiii, 34, 57–58, 65, 70, 76
plans for escape 42–43
playing skills of 14, 18
public speaking xiii, 32, 36–37, 50–51, 53–57, 70–71
reading the Bible 22, 25–26, 51
Rhode Island campaign 60–61
salary/wages 23, 42, 43, 55, 78
schooling on Wye Plantation 17
shift to Lynn 58–59
siblings xii, 4, 11, 13–14, 20, 21, 28 *see also* Bailey, Eliza
support for 53, 58, 59–60, 65, 69
teaching at Sunday school xiii, 31–32
tour with Kelley, Abby xv, 67–71
travels as a speaker xiv, xvi, 54–55, 57–59, 62, 70, 71, 72–79, 83–84
a violinist 40, 52
wife *see* Murray, Anna
work life xiii–xiv, 23, 30–35, 42–43, 47–48
Bailey, Harriet x, xii, 3, 4, 6, 11, 15–16, 20, 21, 41
Bailey, Henny 27, 29
Bailey, Isaac 5–6, 11
Bailey, Jenny x, 2, 4, 6, 11
Bailey, Perry 4, 13–14, 21

Bailey, Sarah 4, 14, 21, 28
Baltimore xii, xiii, xiv, 17, 18, 19–20, 22, 24, 27, 33, 35–42, 44, 47, 52, 54
Baly family/Bailey family, the ix–x, 2, 3, 4–7, 10–16, 20–21
  see also individual members
Barbados ix, x, xx, 1
beating of slaves xii, xiii, 14, 20, 28, 29, 30, 45
  see also whipping
Bethel African Methodist Episcopal Church 25, 36, 70
Bible, the 22, 25, 28, 51
Bjornlund, Lydia 2, 59
Black(s)
  abolitionists 49–50, 69, 79
  church members xiii, 46
  free people xi, xiv, 2, 7, 19, 40, 46, 51, 78
  slaves ix, xi, xiii, 1, 5 *see also* Baly family/Bailey family, the
  women 3, 39, 40–41, 59–60, 64, 85
  workers ix, 34
  see also Negroes/"nigger"
Blight, David 32, 40, 52, 58, 62, 70, 73, 74, 75, 78
bondage 1–3, 25, 31–32, 54, 75, 81
  see also slavery; slave(s)
Boston xi, xii, xvi, 51, 71, 78, 81
  Anti-Sabbath Convention xv, 63
  Anti-Slavery Society xiii, xv, 59, 61, 64, 67, 83

anti-slavery speech in 62
Bound for the Promised Land: Harriet Tubman 2
Bradburn, George xvi, 72, 77
Brazil xx
Bristol County 46, 52, 77
Brown, John x
Buffalo 72, 74–75
Buffum, James N. xvi, 58, 83, 84
Burchard, Peter 6, 12, 19, 40

Cambria (ship) 83–84
Canada xix, 32
Caribbean, the xix, xx
Caroline Street 39, 40, 42
caulkers xiii, xiv, 34, 36, 41, 43, 44, 47, 48
Chapman, Maria W. xi, xii, xiii, 67, 68, 73
chattel 20–21, 54, 77
Chesapeake Bay 2, 10, 82
children xxi, 42
  bi-racial 3, 11–12
  free xi, 38
  slave *see* slave children
Christ, Jesus 63, 78
Civil War 69, 81
Clay, Henry 75
Clinton County 75, 77
Coffin, William C. 52
Coles, Howard W. 76–77
Collins, John A. xv, xvi, 54–55, 56, 57–58, 72, 73, 77
colonization xiv, 51, 52

colored people 6, 16, 28, 35, 36, 50–52, 72
Columbian Orator, The xiii, 23, 26, 32, 53
Congress xii, 35, 49
Connecticut x, xi, 65, 72
Covey, Edward xiii, 30–31, 34, 82
Cox, Ruth xvi, 78–79
creole people 1, 38

Declaration of Independence 51
Deep South xx, 1, 27, 33
DeGruy, Joy xix, xxi, 85
Denton xi, 38
Dorr, Thomas W. 60
Douglass *see* Bailey, Frederick Augustus Washington (Douglass)
Douglass, Charles xvi, 58, 79

East Baltimore [Mental] Improvement Society 36–37
Eastern Shore of Maryland x, 2, 5, 8, 27, 32, 38, 45, 48, 79
Easton xiii, 21, 78
economic slump 27–29
emancipation xi, xii, 33, 38, 49
Emerson, Ralph Waldo 50
E. M. P. Wells School 40, 42
equal rights 54, 68, 84
Erie Canal 70, 72
escapees 16, 44, 46, 67–68
Europe xx, 81
Europeans xix, xx, 1

Fell's Point xii, 18, 34, 37, 42
field hands xiii, 1, 12, 31
Foster, George 54, 56
Foster, Stephen S. xv, 60, 65, 67
Fought, Leigh
   on Auld, Lucretia 17
   Frederick's stint as a servant 42
   Improvement Society membership 37
   on Murray family 39, 41
   public speaking of Douglass 54
   right to a personal life 64
   women in leadership 60, 68
Frederick *see* Bailey, Frederick Augustus Washington (Douglass)
Frederick Douglass' Paper xvii
free Blacks xi, xiv, 2, 7, 19, 40, 46, 51, 78
free colored people 6, 28, 36
freedom xvii, xx, 23, 26, 35, 48, 80
   advocate of 54, 57
   escape to xii, xiii, 16, 32, 44, 46, 51
Freeland, William xiii, 31, 35, 37, 78
fugitives xv, 35, 51, 60, 71, 74, 82

Gardiner, William 34
Garnet, Henry Highland (Rev.) 52, 75
Garrison, William Lloyd 36, 56–58, 82
   Anti-Sabbath Convention xv, 63

anti-slavery movement xi,
    xiii–xvi, 50, 67, 69–73, 78
early life xi
editor of *Liberator, The* xiii, 49
followers/supporters of 54–55,
    58, 62, 69
a newspaper writer xii, xiii
preface writing for the *Narrative* 81
reward for kidnapping of xiii, 49
a speaker 50, 53, 65
Gay, Sidney Howard xvi, 72
Georgia xiii, 27, 49
Goodell, William 72, 74
Great House, the ix, x, xiii, 13–14
Green, Beriah 72
Griffiths, Julia 41

Happy Alley 18, 25, 37
Harari, Yuval Noah xx
Hardy, Neal 76
Hillsboro 17, 20
History of Woman Suffrage, The 61
Holley, Myron 73, 75
Holley, Sally 75
Holme Hill Farm x, xi, 10, 20
Hopper, Anna 67
Hudson, Erasmus 70
Hutchinson Family Singers xvi,
    83–84

Indiana xvi, 59, 65, 72, 75, 77, 80
Ireland 83, 84

James, Thomas (Rev.) xi, 50

Johnson, Frederick *see* Bailey,
    Frederick Augustus Washington
    (Douglass)
Johnson, Nathan 47, 51
Judkins, Captain 84

Katy (Aunt) 15, 17, 20
Kelley, Abby xi, xv, 60, 62, 65,
    67–71, 73

labor/laborer xii, 1, 8, 27, 34, 48,
    51, 58
Larson, Kate Clifford 2
Latimer, George xv, 71
law(s) 61, 74, 83
    on bi-racial children 3, 12
    by colonial owners 2
    on slave meetings 28
    against slave trade xii,
        35, 65
Lawson, Charles 25–26
lawyers 20, 51–52
Liberator, The xiii, xiv, 49, 50, 51, 54,
    55, 71, 75, 81
Liberty Party xvii, 69, 73, 75
*Life and Times of Frederick Douglass
    Written by Himself* 12
Lloyd, Daniel 14, 18
Lloyd family, the 7, 10, 31, 82
    ancestors ix, x, xiii
    plantations 4, 8–9, 13–14,
        17–18, 20
    slaves 5, 12, 13–14 *see also* Baly
        family/Bailey family, the

Lloyd V, Edward (Colonel) x, xiii, 8–9, 12, 13, 14, 17, 31, 82
Lloyd II, Edward ix
Loguen, Jermain Wesley 67–68
London xiv, 1
Loring, Ellis Gray 51–52
Lovejoy, Elijah xiv
Lynn xv, 57–59, 64, 68, 71, 73, 77, 78, 80, 83, 84

McFeely, William 40, 42, 77
Mann, Horace 50
manumission 2
Massachusetts x, xi, 44, 56, 57, 68, 71, 75, 77, 80, 83, 84
   Anti-Slavery Society xv, 52, 53, 54, 59, 72, 76, 78
   Frederick's move to xiv, xv, 46–48, 64
   speeches against slavery 62, 66
   voting tax 52
   see also Lynn; Nantucket; New Bedford
May, Samuel J. (Rev.) 72
meetings
   anti-slavery xv–xvi, 50, 54, 60, 64–65, 67, 70, 80
   disruption of xiii, 28, 59, 70, 73, 77
   "Latimer" 71
   "one hundred conventions" tour 72–79
   prayer/religious 25, 42, 51
   protest 58

Quaker 2, 47
Merryman, John 42
middle class, the xi, 39, 41, 59, 60, 64
Mirror of Liberty xiv, 44
mob 59, 61, 65, 67, 68, 75, 76–77
Monroe, James xv, xvi, 60, 65, 69, 72
Montell, Elizabeth xiii, 38–39
Montell, Francis xiii, 38–39
Mott, Abigail 68–69
Mott, Lucretia C. x, xii, xiii, xiv, xv, 63, 67
Mott, Lydia 68–69
Murray, Anna xiii, 37–42, 65, 73, 78–79
   appearance and dressing 39–40
   birth and childhood 38
   children of xiv, xv, xvi, 5, 52, 58, 79 *see also* Douglass, Charles
   family life in Massachusetts 47, 52, 64
   a housekeeper/maid/domestic 38–40, 41, 47, 59
   marriage to Douglass/Frederick xi, xiv, 40–41, 45
   meeting Douglass xiv, 37, 40, 42
   move to New Bedford 46–48
   shift to Lynn 58–59
   a violinist 40
Murray family, the 38–41
My Bondage and My Freedom 6–7, 15, 23, 28

Nantucket x, xv, 52, 54, 59, 67, 81
Narrative of the Life of Frederick Douglass, an American Slave, Written by Himself xvi, 11, 45, 80, 81
Negroes/"nigger" 30, 35, 51, 60, 76
    see also Black(s)
New Bedford xv, xvi, 44, 45, 46–54, 56, 58, 67, 80
    anti-slavery activism in 49–55
    attitude toward Blacks in 46–48, 50
    family life of Frederick and Anna 47, 52
    Frederick's move to xiv, 46–48
    whaling industry in 46
New England xiii, xiv, xv, xvi, xix, 46, 48, 59, 65, 71, 81, 82
New Hampshire 72, 73, 84
New York City xiv, xvi, 44, 46, 59, 62, 67, 74, 80
New York State xv, xvi, 45, 67, 68, 69, 70, 82
newspapers 19, 44, 58, 70, 81, 82, 84

Ohio xvi, 59, 65, 72, 75, 77
Oneida County 69, 70
orators 54–57, 65, 76, 79, 81
Other Slavery: The Uncovered Story of Indian Enslavement in America, The xix

Parker, Jane Marsh 51, 80
Pendleton 75–76, 77

Pennington, Rev. James W. C. 45
Pennsylvania xvi, 32, 59, 65, 68, 72, 78
Philadelphia xiv, 35, 42, 44, 59, 63, 68, 77
Phillips, Wendell xi, xiv, xv, 57, 65, 71, 78, 80, 81–82
Pillsbury, Parker xv, 53, 60
Pitts, Helen 41
politics 59, 60, 69
Porter, Samuel D. 73
Post, Amy xv, 69–70, 74
Post, Isaac xv, 70, 74
Post Traumatic Slave Syndrome: America's Legacy of Enduring Injury and Healing xix
piracy xii, 35
plantation(s) xii, xx, 56
    Freeland 35, 37
    Lloyd 4, 8–9, 13–14, 17–18, 20
    Skinner ix–x
    in Talbot County 1–2, 4
prejudice, racial xiii, 34, 48, 50, 64, 69, 70, 83
Preston, Dickson J.
    on Anthony, Aaron 10
    on Baly family 4–5, 7, 15–16
    bondage in Maryland 1–3
    books ix, 1
    Frederick's interest in music 40
    on Lloyd family 8, 12
    slave meetings 28
    speaking career of Frederick 37

Quaker(s), the 58, 74, 78
   abolitionists xv, 60, 68
   meetings 2, 47
   minister xii, xv, 63 *see also* Mott, Lucretia C.
   and slave ownership x, 2
   town 59
   white xi, 46, 53, 60–61
   women xii, 68–70

racism xv, xvi, 34, 58
railroads 16, 35, 57–58, 70, 77
Remond, Charles xv, xvi, 71, 72–75, 77, 79
Reséndez, Andrés xix
Rhode Island xiv, xv, 45, 47, 59, 60–61, 62, 65, 68
Rochester xv, 39–40, 51, 69–70, 73–74, 80, 82
Ruggles, David xi, xiv, 44–45, 46
Rush, Christopher (Bishop) 50

Sabbath school 28, 31
St. Michaels xiii, 27–28, 31
Sally Lloyd (sloop) 17, 38
Sapiens: A Brief History of Humankind xx
servant(s) ix–x, xx, 1, 12, 14, 18, 42
Siebert, Wilbur. H. 42
Skinner, Ann 10
Skinners, the ix–x, 4, 10
slave children 1, 2, 5–7, 13–14
   bi-racial 3, 11–12
   clothing 6, 12
   family circle and values 4, 6, 7
   food 6, 12, 15, 28
   selling of 16, 27, 28
"Slaveholder's Sermon" 62
slave owners x, xx–xxi, 1–2, 4–14, 54, 64
   see also Anthony, Aaron (Captain); Lloyd family, the
slave trade x, xii, xix–xx, 16, 27, 28, 35, 38, 65
slavery ix–xvii
   African x, xix–xxi, 65
   by birth xi, xii, 38
   escape from xii, xiii, 16, 32, 35, 44, 46, 51
   speeches against xiv–xvi, 22, 50–51, 53–55, 62, 65–66, 70, 72–79
   see also anti-slavery movement; slave(s)
slave(s)
   beating/whipping of xii, xiii, 14, 20, 28, 29, 30, 45
   Black ix, xi, xiii, 1, 5
   catchers 44, 56
   codes ix, xx–xxi
   families 1–2, 4–7 *see also* Baly family/Bailey family, the
   food of 6, 12, 15, 28
   fugitive 35, 51, 60, 74, 82
   harsh treatment of xii, xiii, 2, 8, 17, 29, 30
   holders/holdings 10, 12, 31, 48, 62, 82, 84

labor xii, 1, 8
meetings *see* meetings
monetary value of 11, 20–21, 76–77
overseers 4, 8, 9, 31
ownership *see* slave owners
salary of 7
women 1–3, 12, 45 *see also* Bailey, Betsey; Bailey, Harriet
workers 4, 10 *see also* workers
Smith, Gerrit xvii, 72, 73
Smith, James McCune xi, 49–50, 62
South Carolina xi, xx
Sprague, Rosetta Douglass 64
Stanton, Elizabeth Cady xiv, xv, 61, 62
steamboat xiv, 35, 44, 45
Strawberry Alley 25, 37
Sumner, Charles 50
Sunday school xiii, 32
Syracuse 67, 72, 73, 74, 76

Talbot County ix–x, xi, xiii, 1–2, 4, 10, 14, 21, 78, 82
temperance xii, 70
tobacco ix, x, 1, 8
Tompkins County 70
travel(s) xii, xiv, xvi, 1, 32, 54–55, 57–59, 69–71, 73–74, 77–78, 83–84
Tubman, Harriet xii
Tuckahoe Creek x, 5–6, 13, 16, 20, 38

Union Street 58, 80
United Kingdom 81
upstate New York xvi, 65, 69
Utica 69, 73

Vermont 72, 73, 80
Virginia ix, xix, xx, xxi
Virginia Slave Code of 1705, The xx–xxi

Ward, Samuel R. 69
Washington, Booker T. 30–36
  abolitionists' undertaking 72
  apprenticeship of Douglass 34
  Buffalo convention 74–75
  Clinton County meeting 75–76
  Douglass as a speaker 50–51, 53, 54, 56–57, 65–66, 80–81
  escape attempt of Frederick 32, 33
  Improvement Society membership of Douglass 36
  racial discrimination of Frederick 50
  rebellion by Frederick 30
  Rhode Island campaign 60
  slave-holders and nonslave-holders 48
  teaching of slaves 31–32
Webb, Richard D. 84
Wells, Elizabeth 40, 42
Wells, Peter 39
West Indians 1, 5
West Indies xx, 1, 38, 65

Weston, Maria *see* Chapman, Maria W.
whipping xii, 14, 17, 29, 30
White, William A. 65, 76, 77
white(s) ix–xi, xiii, 23, 28
   abolitionists 51, 52, 53, 83
   caulkers 34, 47
   farmers ix, x, 8–9, 31 *see also* Lloyd family, the
   prejudice, racial xiii, 34, 48, 50, 64, 69, 70, 83
   Quakers xi, 46, 53, 60–61
   servants ix–x
   slave-holders and nonslave-holders 48
   women xi, 3, 41, 54, 59–60, 61, 64, 69
women
   abolitionists 58, 60–61, 67–68 *see also* Kelley, Abby; Mott, Lucretia C.
   black 3, 39, 40–41, 59–60, 64, 85
   leaders 60–61, 68
   lecturers 61, 68–69 *see also* Kelley, Abby
   middle-class xi, 39, 41, 60, 64
   Quaker xii, 68–70
   role in the abolition movement 50, 59–61
   slave 1–3, 12, 45 *see also* Bailey, Betsey; Bailey, Harriet
   white xi, 3, 41, 54, 59–60, 61, 64, 69
Women in the World of Frederick Douglass 17
Women of Colonial America 2
Woodard, Colin xx
workers ix, 1, 4, 10, 12, 17, 22, 28, 31, 34, 46, 64
Wright, Paulina 69
Wye House ix, x, xiii, 13–14
Wye Plantation 13, 17–18

Young Frederick Douglass, The Maryland Years ix, 1, 7

Zion chapel xiv, 50

www.ingramcontent.com/pod-product-compliance
Lightning Source LLC
Chambersburg PA
CBHW021115080526
44587CB00010B/525